BRISTOL HISTORY WALKS

BARB DRUMMOND

Copyright © 2023 by Barb Drummond

All rights reserved.

No part of this book may be reproduced in any form or by any electronic or mechanical means, including information storage and retrieval systems, without written permission from the author, except for the use of brief quotations in a book review.

By the same author:

Frolicksome Women & Troublesome Wives: Wife Selling in England

Mr Bridges' Enlightenment Machine: Forty Years on Tour in Georgian England

The Midas of Manumission: The Orphan Samuel Gist And His Virginian Slaves

barbdrummond@hotmail.com

www.barbdrummondcurioushistorian.com

Paperback ISBN 978-1-912829-12-5

ebook 978-1-912829-13-2

❧ Created with Vellum

"In a dark bottom sunk, O Bristol! now
    With native malice lift thy low'ring brow;
    Then as some hell-born sprite in mortal guise
    Borrows the shape of Goodness and belies,
    All fair, all smug, to yon' proud hall invite,
    To feast all strangers an air polite"

Thy sons! tho' crafty, def to Wisdom's call,
    Despising all men, and despised by all ;
    Sons! while thy cliffs a ditch-like river laves,
    Rude as thy rocks, and muddy as thy waves,
    Of thoughts as narrow as of words immense,
    As full of turbulence as void of sense?"
- Richard Savage

When I have a little money, I buy books; and if I have any left, I buy food and clothes.

DESIDERIUS ERASMUS ROTERODAMUS

CONTENTS

A Brief History of Bristol	xi
Instructions For Walks	xlix
Chapter 1	1
Chapter 2	12
Chapter 3	22
Chapter 4	34
Chapter 5	52
Chapter 6	62
Chapter 7	80
Chapter 8	90
Chapter 9	102
Chapter 10	112
Chapter 11	122
Chapter 12	132
Chapter 13	140
References/Further Reading	147
About the Author	149

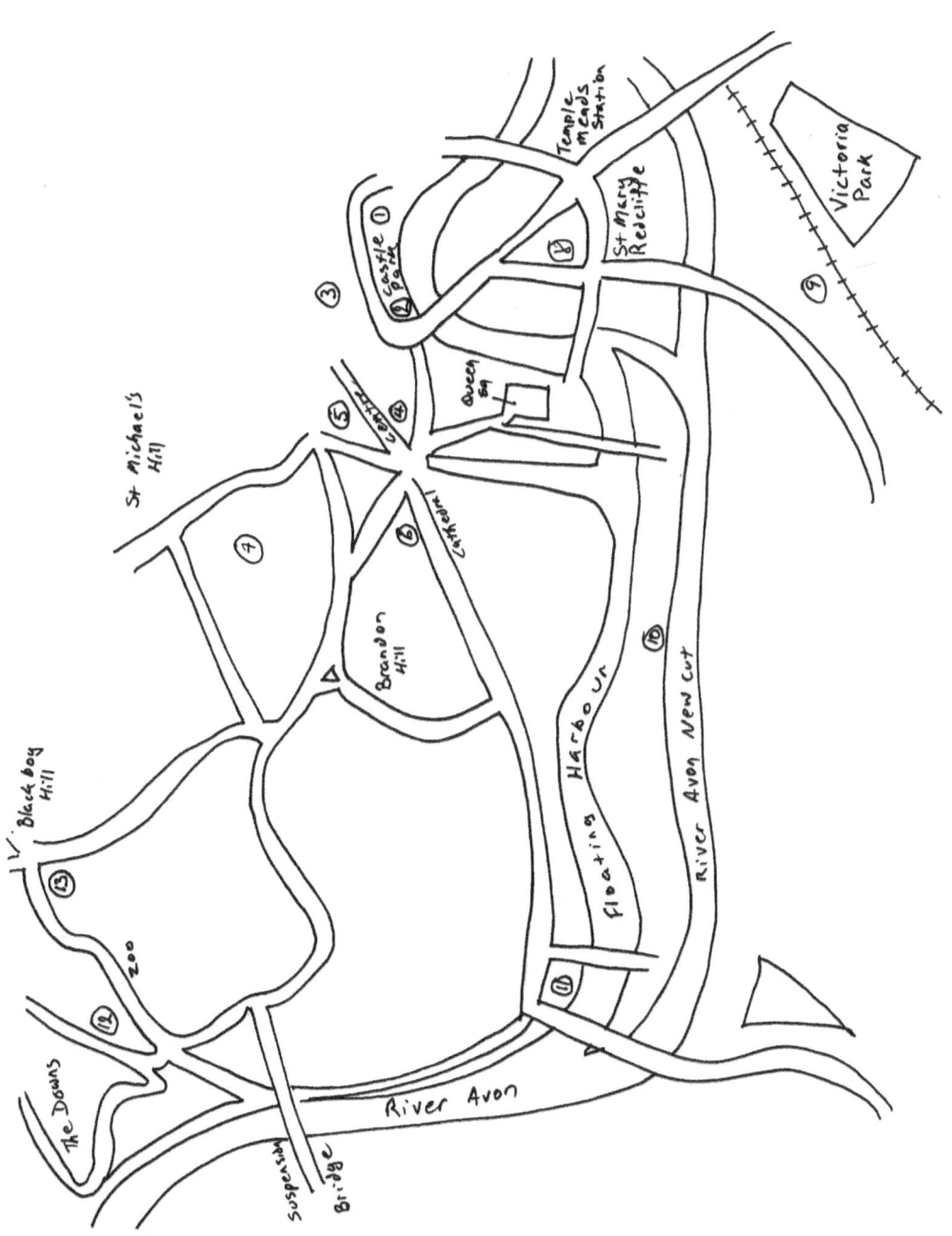

A BRIEF HISTORY OF BRISTOL

Introduction

The origins of the city of Bristol are obscure. The earliest known settlements were downstream at a crossing on the River Avon. Fortifications were on the heights near the future Brunel's Suspension Bridge . Evidence of Roman settlements were found along the River Trym, and the port of Abona was at its junction with the Avon. The oldest archeological finds in Bristol itself are some pieces of Roman lead. The nearest religious house was at Westbury-on-Trym which was part of the See of Worcester.

The first evidence of the city's name ending in 'l' comes from the reign of Henry I. The Latin Bristowia may have been anglicised to Bristolia. The thriving settlement is often called a city but the term is not strictly accurate until Henry VIII decreed the founding of a new diocese, making its abbey a cathedral in 1542.

The first person of note was St Wulfstan, Bishop of Worcester. He preached against the sale of English slaves to the Norse who had settled in Ireland. It was common practice to keep foreign slaves as they were unable to run away. They were sold at what is now Old Market in Gloucestershire, beyond control of the town. The Normans established markets within walking distance of settlements to ensure food supplies. Further links with Ireland are found in Camden who claimed that under Henry II a colony of Bristol settled in Dublin and were granted "all the liberties and free customs which those of Bristol enjoyed". Given Ireland's later history this seems odd, especially with the comment "which perhaps at that time was drained of inhabitants". The 18th century historian Dr Barratt claimed that Henry II, as soon as he granted Bristol's burgesses their first charter also granted them the city of Dublin.

Bristol's wealth soared in the thirteenth century, mostly from the international wool trade, and from cod fishing. This led to the uniting the two regions to build three massive civil engineering works. The town was called 'the place of the bridge' in Saxon. This could have meant a landing stage, but it was more likely a causeway or ford for crossing at low tide. The earliest evidence of a stone bridge was the construction a four-arch structure in the thirteenth century. The River Frome was rerouted from modern Baldwin Street to St Augustine's Reach, and the Saxon walls were rebuilt further out.In the centre of the bridge was the Chapel of the Assumption, dedicated in 1361. The borders of St Nicholas and St Thomas parishes ran down the centre of the bridge, but the chapel was in the former. It was funded by the burgesses of both sides of the Avon, and the Pope granted them the rights to ring bells and hold services there, similar to the chapel of St Thomas on London Bridge. It straddled the bridge and a central gateway. Its buttressed tower of one hundred feet was the tallest in the town and was supported by a pillar or cutwater upstream. It is described by Pevsner as "quite ambitious". Locally born chronicler William of Worcestre described it in c.1600. It was in the decorated gothic style, with vaults. Its' four-light traceried windows held painted glass which showed the donors at its base. This is the only record of stained glass in the town at the time. Donations by worshippers maintained the bridge and probably also the seven which crossed the Frome, most of which survive beneath the city centre. Soon after the bridge was built, it became lined with shops with houses above, supported by secondary arches. With so much passing traffic, they were prime real estate. In 1646 a fire broke out in an apothecary's shop which destroyed many properties. They were rebuilt with timber and lead from Raglan Castle and its woods, the last of the royalist defences to fall.

By the 1730s houses had built shopfronts which encroached on the roadway, and rising traffic made the bridge dangerous for pedestrians, i.e., the poor. It was rebuilt in the 1760s by the aptly named James Bridges. He followed the design and techniques of the Swiss-born clockmaker/engineer Labelye on Westminster Bridge. Instead of rerouting the Avon, as for the original, he floated caissons into place which allowed masons to work underwater. Bridges was a talented engineer and architect whose presence in the city raised standards. But he was treated with contempt by the bridge Trustees. He left before completing the bridge and the rebuilding of St Nicholas's church. Both were finished by his colleague, the carver/mason Thomas Paty.

Mismanagement of the tolls over succeeding decades led to a riot on 28 September 1793. It was described as "the most tragical local incident of the century" and a foretaste of the 1831 riots. The toll houses were demolished in 1861 and the addition of a steel parapet in the 1960s "completed the desecration".

After Bristol Bridge was rebuilt, Bridge Street was laid out to provide access to it. New houses were planned to generate income to help pay for the bridge building. It led to Peter Street which ran past the front of the church, which continued to Union Street. Both streets were laid out by Thomas Paty. He was the most successful of a family who dominated the city's eighteenth century building trade. Their name appeared in the 1720s with a James Paty freestone mason on Old King Street, now Merchant Street. Thomas and his brother, another James, lived in St Augustine's parish. Thomas had a house and yard near the central library and James was in Denmark St. They sometimes competed with each other for contracts. On large projects James did the heavy work in the mid to late eighteenth century. Thomas was a fine carver and his memorials can be found across the city, throughout South Gloucestershire and in the West Indies. His sons John and William were students at Queen Elizabeth Hospital.

They were the city's first graduates from the Royal Academy. The former was a carver, the latter an architect. The family's designs have been called dull, but Bristol was a working city, so their output was dictated by their patrons, who were mostly merchants. Bristol's economy, and its architecture is thus very different from nearby Bath, the Las Vegas of its age. Their business was unique in surviving the Napoleonic financial crash to continue under other names well into the twentieth century.

Following the Seven Years War which established the United Kingdom as Europe's major naval power, Bristol's population soared and the city expanded into new streets and terraces, especially on the heights of Kingsdown and Clifton. Estimates have been made that in 1757 there were thirteen thousand houses, which rose to ninety thousand, so was similar to London within its walls.

The Castle

The first castle may have been a Saxon wooden fort built to protect the port or river crossing before it was replaced by the Normans. An archeological dig of 1948 on Castle Green found 12th century pottery and a well. John Leland was told it was built of Caen stone. It comprised eleven acres, so was one of the largest castles in England. Its keep was one of the finest, occupying over half the present park and extending to Old Market roundabout. As a royal property, it was exempt from taxes so was not included in The Domesday Book.

But by the 15th century, the use of gunpowder in bombardments made castles redundant. When Elizabeth visited the city she stayed at John Young's Great House beyond St John's Gate instead. When William of Worcester visited in 1480, the castle was already locked up and decaying. He recorded the keep at 60 by 45 feet, with walls of 25 foot at the base, and towers at each corner. The hall was 36 yards by 18, with 14 foot high walls and a pitched roof with 45 foot long rafters. Near the keep was a chapel of St Martin, patron saint of soldiers.

The castle had 4 gates. Eastgate was blocked in the 13th century. Newgate survived into the 18th century as a debtors' prison. Early

Quakers bribed the keeper to let them pass out of the city to attend their Sunday services in Broadmead. Barbican Gate was above the Sallyport. Another gate led to a bridge over Castle Ditch to Queen Street.

The main builder of what are now the castle ruins was the Bishop of Coutances. He established it as a royal stronghold to dominate the trading port, so the first castle probably predates Domesday. The town's wealth was similar to York, Lincoln and Norwich. But physically it was more like pre-industrial Birmingham or Manchester, with significant trade but little political power. Robert of Gloucester built the huge stone keep in 1120–30 on top of the old foundations. It was similar to London and Rochester. It was the country's greatest keep.

There were rumbling disputes between King Edward II — or rather, his various sheriffs — and the increasingly wealthy, independent townspeople. This led locals to demand more power. Following the murder of one of the constable's men in 1312, the townsmen refused to hand over the culprit. They built a wall to lay siege to the castle and began The Great Insurrection. Constables from nearby counties were drawn into the dispute which lasted till May 1313. The troublemakers were not pardoned till 1322. An inquiry led to a riot at the Guildhall which resulted in twenty deaths. This probably accelerated the move towards Bristol becoming a town and county in 1373, when their sheriff took on most of the constable's duties.

In 1327 Edward was imprisoned in Bristol Castle but moved to Berkeley on 5 April, Palm Sunday. He was tortured to death to avoid signs of murder. His body was offered to Bristol Abbey and the priests of Malmesbury and Kingswood, but they refused for fear of offending the queen. Gloucester Abbey accepted his body and their abbot benevolently collected it in his own carriage. Until The Reformation, it attracted large numbers of pilgrims and their offerings.

Town and City

Bristol's land is rocky with thin soil and from early times it needed to import its food. But it was the only region in southern England with nearby coalfields. So it was a very early site of manufacturing before the Industrial Revolution.

Like the nearby Wye, the River Avon was a source of salmon and eels which were used as food and as currency to pay land rents. Its huge tidal range drove ships into the port, aided by prevailing south west winds. But those winds also delayed departures, especially of troops, who sometimes became so bored they rioted. To overcome this, Hungroad was, three miles down stream, now Shirehampton, and Kingroad, now Pill, had a good open harbour and safe anchorage. Both were often used for arrivals and departures. People and goods travelled from the city by rowing boats or overland.

The town of Bristol was built on high ground. Archaeological remains show floods fourteen foot above the high tide mark in the thirteenth century. In 1244 the town was granted the right to trade throughout England, Normandy and Wales without tolls or taxes. In 1247 a charter extended these rights to the southern parishes, allowing the northern parishes to demand they pay half the costs of the rerouting of the Avon and the building of what appears to be the first stone bridge uniting them. They were granted equal trading rights in return. Bristol became a county with a charter granting the right to transact its own legal affairs in 1373, taking on powers previously held by the king. This meant they owed no allegiance to aristocrats, so became freemen. The document praised Bristol merchants for their shipping and confirmed their rights south of the bridge, challenging the power of the Berkeley family. The town was also granted county status, for a sheriff to hold court. This gave them legal independence from justices of Gloucestershire and Somerset, saving them time and money. They celebrated by the erection of the first High Cross at the town's main crossroads of High, Corn, Broad and Wine Streets. It was a delicate tabernacle with niches for statues of the monarchs who granted these rights. Another tier was added in Charles I's reign.

In 1441 The Royal Court of the Tolzey was annexed to the town, granting it control of Old Market via the Pie Powder Court beyond the town gates. This was another huge advance in the town's rights and powers. In 1446 Bristol was excluded from the Court of Admiralty. This allowed the mayor and recorder to control maritime affairs. This, including piracy, far beyond the town limits to Portishead, Walton-in-Gordano and Weston-super-Mare. But the castle with its gardens and orchards to the east were not included, remaining an enclave of Gloucestershire. It was a haven for criminals and 'sly traders', debtors and 'sturdy beggars', swindlers, thieves, highwaymen and malefactors of every description. They defied the officers of justice and preyed with impunity upon the town and surrounding districts. They were too far from Gloucester justices and immune to those of Bristol, like London's infamous Holbourne Liberty.

By 1480 the post of constable was a mere sinecure. He profited by renting properties, but failed to enforce standards which led to rising numbers of hovels. From 1611 the city council tried to end the danger in their midst. Charles agreed after hearing claims that men hiding there to avoid being drafted as soldiers. In 1629 a charter was granted to separate the region from Gloucester to become part of Bristol.

Bristol Corporation purchased the precinct in 1630, taking control of law enforcement and taxation. Its open spaces were soon transformed into streets, and the income for St Peters Parish increased. But only 37 honest residents were admitted as freemen. A few years later, several armed companies, i.e., local militia, kept their weapons in the Artillery House they had built there. The castle was almost demolished.

In 1630 Charles I granted a charter which separated the castle and precincts from the county of Gloucestershire, bringing it under control of Bristol. This prevented any officer of Gloucestershire interfering in the area, and all inhabitants were able to become freemen of Bristol. Though lands remained in crown ownership, the mayor was in charge. In 1631 the Castle precincts were at last separated from the crown at a cost of £959.

Whenever a monarch was crowned, the city requested their town charter be renewed. In 1684 Charles II confirmed the city and county with the same boundaries. The mayor's rights were continued, to regulate markets, and three fairs per year for wool on King Street, and five others for horses etc in January on Temple Street, March and

November on Redcliffe Hill, November in Broadmead, and September on Temple Street. All were to be regulated via the Pie Powder Court.

Religious Houses

Bristol has long prided itself on its independence from feudal lordships, but the Berkeley family played a major role in the region and the town. The family is almost unique in English history. It has an unbroken line of descent from noble Angles and Saxons who survived the Norman invasion. They still hold much of the land they acquired in 1066 which includes Berkley Castle in South Gloucestershire. They played an important role as landowners and founders of charities in the region.

The manor of Berkeley was given to Roger de Berkeley of Dursley at the Conquest. But the third of that name supported Stephen, so lost the estates. The lands were granted to Robert Fitzharding who died c.1170, a wealthy merchant and Reeve of Bristol. 'Fitz' means he was illegitimate. He obtained the manor of Berkeley in 1135 where he built the castle which the family still owns. He was the son of a Bristol magistrate named Harding when William the Conqueror arrived. He became an important official under Edward the Confessor. The family's estates were huge; their thirty parishes made them one of the largest landowners in England. Their role in law enforcement and charity cannot be underestimated. The wealth of the wool trade also made them some of the richest and most powerful figures of the time. For many centuries, the wealth of England was dependent on sheep. The Berkeleys ruled most of the land that produced the wool to the north of the city and housed the supporting industries.

The family also promoted education and the arts. In 1384 Dame Katherine Berkeley founded England's first grammar school at Wotton-under-Edge. She believed many people wished to learn grammar, "which is the foundation of all other liberal arts, is often frustrated through poverty". William Tyndale and Edward Jenner were pupils. The family held lands in the south of Bristol and founded three important charities. In 1200 they built St John's Hospital opposite St Mary Redcliffe church for brothers and sisters of the Augustinian order in Redcliffe Pit to care for the sick and the poor, but its land has been mostly engulfed by the nearby roundabout. A chapel is shown on eighteenth century maps in the centre of the churchyard. In 1571 Queen Elizabeth gave the chapel to the parish as a free grammar and writing school which was swept away by improvements. The school continued in the east end of the church, now St Mary's chapel.

The Reformation provided a surge in wealth from the sale of church property. In Bristol this allowed the city gates and quays to become toll free till well into the 18th century. The replacement of church charities was left to locals who founded new institutions such as hospitals, schools snd almshouses for the poor.

St Katherine's Brightbow was a hospital founded by Robert de Berkeley about 1200 between Bedminster and Redcliffe. St Mary Magdalene was a nearby women's leper hospital. The region was low lying and marshy, with Brightbow Bridge crossing the Malago stream and part of the road to Bristol was a causeway.

Robert Fitzharding, later the first Lord Berkeley, founded the Abbey of St Augustine in the 12th century. The family added the chapter house and in the 13th century the Lady Chapel. At the Reformation, it became Bristol Cathedral. A relative, Maurice de Gaunt, established a monastic foundation across what is now College Green. Under his nephew Robert de Gournay it became Gaunt's Hospital. In 1541 the church was sold to the city corporation for £1,000. It is still the only civic-owned church in England. The rest became the Queen Elizabeth Hospital to house and educate orphaned sons of freemen.

Robert Fitzharding is buried in the Benedictine Priory of St James. This was probably the first of the town's many religious houses. His family was powerful before the Norman Conquest, and was significant as they were bourgeois rather than feudal. Fitzharding's wife Eva founded the small house of the white-gowned Austin canonesses on St Michael's Hill. It was dedicated to St Mary Magdalene and funded by lands at Southmead. The order gave their name to Whiteladies Road, which is often assumed to be linked to the Atlantic slave trade. This is nonsense as at the time all 'ladies' were aristocrats, hence white, so this would be a tautology. Opposite Clifton Down Shopping Centre is Whiteladies Gate. The corner shop shows statues of the monarchs who supported the charity. They include Kings John and Henry II, and Queens Eleanor and Isabella. Thus it long predates Atlantic slavery.

The town and its growing population expanded north of the Avon towards Kingsdown in the Middle Ages. The people were served by three friaries and St Michael's parish church. The new parish of St James was established in 1374 when the priory was extended and reroofed to serve the populous industrial region.

The origins and early history of St Mary Redcliffe, to the south are obscure. It was first recorded c.1160, and rebuilding of much of the church began in 1340, but was halted by the Black Death. It was eventually rebuilt in the pared-down Perpendicular Gothic style, like most of the region's churches, the result of the manpower shortage. But it had the grand design of an abbey, not a parish church. It is often wrongly claimed to have been funded by merchant prince Canynge.

St Bartholomew's was a small hospital at the bottom of Christmas Steps for poor men and women and its lands stretched up the hill to those of the Magdalenes. It was founded c.1230–40 by the de la Warr branch of the Berkeley family and they were still patrons at the dissolution of the monasteries. It was converted c.1538 for the use of Bristol Grammar School. But in the early 18th century, it swapped premises with Queen Elizabeth's Hospital.

Bristol's population grew during the reign of Henry III (1216–72). This increased the town's ability to fund religious houses, but it also created a rising need for charities to support the poor. The town became encircled by large, well-funded monastic institutions. With the town surrounded by hills, these religious houses built conduits to provide clean water. Benedictine monks were at St James' Priory by c.1134, then Augustan canons built St Augustan's Abbey. The Dominicans settled at Blackfriars. It was founded in 1220 by Maurice de Gaunt beside the River Frome, opposite the castle. Henry III donated oaks from a royal forest and provided a conduit from the royal manor of Barton Regis. In 1230 St Bartholomew's Hospital was founded.

Franciscans or Grey Friars settled in Lewin's Mead, with a pipe from St Michael's Hill, the only conduit to survive. The house of the Carmelites or White Friars house was founded by Edward III in 1267 and became the town's largest and finest religious house. Its nave was nine hundred feet long, and its long, slender steeple had a 200 foot tower. Its tiled pavement showed tilting knights. It is now the site of the Beacon arts venue, formerly Colston Hall.

The town was surrounded by hills, and the houses built conduits to provide clean water. Friars were not funded by wealthy magnates, so they survived by begging and probably sold the produce of their gardens and beehives.

The first of the religious houses to fall under Henry VIII's reforms was the Magdalene nunnery in 1536. It was then surviving on just £21 per year, with only an elderly prioress and a novice remaining. From 1537, the 4 friaries of the Carmelites, Franciscans, Augustans and finally the Dominicans all fell. Only the Augustan prior held on till the end. All the orders also had to surrender the lands which supported them, with the Benedictines at St James' Priory being the last. Religious Guilds had often met in church crypts. They helped fund the church buildings and maintain standards, and provided charity for their members. Many survived as secular trade companies, still called guilds.

The corporation melted down much of the church plate in a mint which provided coins to buy the church lands. St Stephen's church produced an astonishing 1,000 ounces of silver plate, as well as vestments such as copes and chasubles. With these riches, the corporation funded the purchase of the town's religious houses to free the town of their tolls. Plate from the western shires was also destroyed here, though many of the coins they made were soon debased.

It is hard to know how much Bristolians opposed Henry VIII's Reformation. Merchants tended to be pragmatic. The city's extensive trade with Spain probably limited its support for reform. The city's residents were also deeply attached to their parish churches, most of which they funded and chose their own clergy. By contrast, in London and the eastern counties, were closer to Protestant Europe and less reliant on Catholic trade. To them, the Reformation was often welcomed as a chance to plunder church property.

At the Reformation, Bristol was home to eighteen parish churches, many of which were founded in the twelfth century. But this compares poorly with towns such as its medieval rival wool town of Norwich which had 43, and with York, with 39. The Reformation put an end to church building, so by the early 18th century, many were in a very poor state.

The number and range of religious buildings in the city has expanded since the eighteenth century to include Catholic chapels, synagogues and mosques.

Roman Catholics

Only one non-resident Catholic priest and five Protestant artisans died under Mary's attempts to restore Catholicism. No priests were hanged under Elizabeth. However, in Bristol Roman followers were harassed and persecuted, especially during the mayoralty of Sir John Knight. There was no Catholic gentry nearby to hide or protect priests or worshippers. In the reign of Charles II, it was claimed that a Fleming had sheltered a priest and celebrated masses for many sailors in the port. In the early years of the eighteenth century, many of Bristol's industries imported skilled people from Europe. Some were Catholics from the Austrian Netherlands and the Rhineland who insisted on freedom of worship. So a chapel was founded at Baptist Mills, which Wesley described as a centre of Catholicism. In 1716 a priest was arrested but then released on a promise of good behaviour. It seems the city tolerated such lawbreaking if it served the expansion of the city's industries and commerce, but this was never guaranteed.

The first Catholic priest in Bristol after the Reformation was Father John Scudamore, a Jesuit of Monmouth, who prepared the ground for those who followed. The Jesuits were called the Janissaries of the Reformation, so were often the first to settle. But Baptist Mills was too far away to serve the city and visitors to the Hotwells. In the 1760s an attempt to establish a mass house was discovered beyond the city limits at the spa, and those involved were 'admonished'. It was still illegal to celebrate mass, and for a Romish priest to dwell in any

English city. Yet Henry Carew was accused of being a priest whilst holding the post of surveyor at the Customs House.

The town clerk sent the government a list of the professions of Catholics in Bristol. It covered a wide range of occupations, including tailors, a shipwright, weaver, gardener and "a stranger". Ships' crews were always multinational and multicultural, so likely numbered many of the old faith. If a Bristol sailor died or fled in a foreign port, there would have been little concern about the religion of his replacement.

From the 1740s, the aforementioned Father John Scudamore served from a chapel above a warehouse on St James Back (now Silver Street in the city centre). By c.1800 priests fleeing Napoleon were in Bristol. They were probably accepted as fellow enemies of the French. Some supported themselves by teaching French. When St Joseph's Chapel on Trenchard Street opened in 1790, its congregation were granted legal rights to say public masses. Probably due to Irish immigration, it soon needed larger premises. It is now Grade II listed, named Chapel House and owned by the Church of England. By the mid-nineteenth century, the new Catholic parish began building a pro-cathedral in Clifton. But this ran into structural and financial problems, so the community bought St Mary-on-the Quay from the Irvingite sect. St Joseph's continued operation till 1871 when it became St Mary's school. Only the Gothic facade survives, with enclosed garden.

In 1777 Father John Fountaine succeeded Scudamore and began the registers which show the variety within the local Catholic community. It included brass-workers and sailors. Irish people had long fled to Bristol from poverty at home. Their numbers surged when many found work building the Floating Harbour in the early 19th century. The Catholic Relief Act was passed in 1791. In 1831 the senior priest was Father Edgeworth. He was a Franciscan, an order known for their teaching and charitable work. This suggests their community was well established. Edgeworth was a great promoter of reform and a member of the Philosophical and Literary Institution.

Nonconformists

The near-lawless enclave of the seventeenth century Castle Precincts allowed freedom of worship for those who rejected the Book of Common Prayer. The city's first Nonconformist congregation began there. The parish churches were independently managed, so able to change with the times. William Yeamans was the vicar of St Philips which adjoined the castle. He led services without 'The Book of Common Prayer'. Dorothy Hazard's first husband was Anthony Kelly, a grocer on High Street whose group of worshippers gathered in the castle. On his death his wife continued his business and his practice of opening on holy days. She married Matthew Hazard who became vicar of the small parish of St Ewen's. Their house was a haven for emigrants on their way to complete the Reformation in New England. With 4 others, she organised the first non-Anglican congregation in Bristol. They stayed within the law by attending divine service at St Ewen's after their own services. These tentative rebellions were warnings of what was to come. Hazard must have been popular, as he is listed as vicar of St Mary Redcliffe when in 1639 William Noble was 'ejected' and Hazard 'intruded' where he remained until 1660.

The number of Nonconformist chapels surged during the Civil War. Many of their members were wealthy. This enabled them to fund their own meeting houses, as well as pay for the maintenance of Anglican 'steeple houses' and clergy. Castle Green was the earliest independent chapel, founded in 1652. The Baptists began in The Friars and expanded to The Pithay before flourishing at Old King Street (now Merchant Street).

After the Civil War and the Restoration of the Monarchy, Royalists such as William Colston served on the city council. The Conventicles Acts were used to harass Nonconformists. Sir John Knight (one of several of that name, which has caused much confusion) was mayor in 1663-4. He vowed not just to extirpate Nonconformity itself, but its very name in the region. He made full use of the draconian Acts which were originally aimed at exposing Roman Catholics. His allies were Bishop Carleton, the lawyer John Helier and innkeeper Ralph Oliffe. Unsurprisingly, Knight had spent time in the West Indies, and a

Heliar's family probably owned Jamaican estates. Knight, Helier and the infamous Bristol mob raided meetings, arrested worshippers and destroyed their furniture and buildings. Oliffe treated the mob with free food and drink to celebrate afterwards. Magistrates imposed fines and, if these went unpaid, imprisoned or transported the victims to the West Indies. Claims were made of ten waves of attacks between 1660 and 1668. Several Nonconformists died from their violence, or from disease in prison. This included the minister John Thompson who died in Newgate.

By 1674 all Bristol's Nonconformist houses were locked up. This forced congregations to meet in the open air at Kingswood, Durdham Down, Baptist Mills and Brislington Common. Some meetings allegedly attracted 1,000 people. But this put them at risk of the county justices. Somerset's were more aggressive than those in Gloucestershire. Several people drowned fleeing the authorities.

Nonconformists refused to swear the Oath of Supremacy. This prevented them from becoming freemen, running businesses in the city, voting and holding public office. Nonetheless, many Nonconformist groups grew in numbers as their members grew in wealth. Their rejection of luxuries provided more money to invest in businesses. But the need to pay fines may have spurred on their business successes.

By 1685 congregations were meeting at Castle Green, Broadmead and The Pithay. John Weekes, an ejected Anglican minister, led a group that eventually settled in Lewins' Mead. By the late 18th century there were Presbyterians in Bridge Street. They moved to Clifton Down where they became extinct. Some of the Castle Green congregation expanded to a fashionable Greek-style chapel in Brunswick Square in 1834–5. In 1837 they held the country's first Nonconformist wedding.

Baptists were probably the largest Nonconformist group in the city. By 1914 they were rebuilding their training college near the university which became independent of the church. Congregationalists also thrived and had a training college for ministers by 1752, but it migrated round the West of England until its return to the city in

1901. As congregations and their wealth grew, they followed the Anglicans out into the healthy suburbs.

Quakers

Barratt claims the first Quaker arrived in the city in 1653. From 1654 they had become the most visible and important Nonconformist group, despite the fact that they were ever very numerous. Perhaps 600 at most attended their monthly meetings. But they punched well above their weight in the fields of wealth, industry and welfare work. In their movement's early years, they were noisy and disrupted church services so they were banned from the cathedral and urban centres. This drove them to preach in open fields and orchards. In 1656 John Naylor's arrival in the city caused outrage because of the blasphemous behaviour of himself and his followers. He was arrested by the mayor and sent to London for trial after which he was repeatedly tortured.

Quakers met in the upper rooms of premises in Broadmead before building their first meeting house in the outer suburb of Frenchay. They met at The Friars in 1670, hence the region's confusing name of Quakers Friars. William Penn married Hannah Callowhill there in 1696, and a Bristolian called James Logan sailed to Pennsylvania as Penn's secretary.

The group built a new house in Temple in 1694 which later became the city's first modern synagogue. Other Quakers settled in surrounding Gloucestershire and Somerset. The Quakers founded their own school in 1668 and contributed to the Sidcot School in Somerset. They lived beyond the old city limits and many became successful in fields such as shipbuilding and metal working. While the Goldney, Darby and Reynolds families ran the ironworks of Coalbrookdale and other businesses in the Midlands, the Champions smelted copper and brass along the River Avon, which led them into engineering. They founded the first china works in the old castle precinct. Several generations of Farleys were involved in newspapers, Harfords were in iron smelting and banking, Fry's made chocolates, and Lloyds were in banking and business. Quakers were also initially involved in the Atlantic slave trade, but they had withdrawn from it by the mid-18th century and became prominent abolitionists. In the USA they were the main group who helped runaway slaves. Their rejection of luxury gave them time and money to devote to charity in general.

Methodists

Preacher George Whitfield was among the earliest Methodists accused of 'enthusiasm', a term usually applied to Catholics, but the meaning of which has long intrigued this author. The excitement of the crowds was at odds with the strict rules of Anglican worship at the time. The Bishop of Bristol John Newton, commenting in the 1760s complained: "Only a bastard form of Popery, Methodism, has troubled Bristol". This 'enthusiasm' has died out in the UK but still thrives in parts of the USA, probably the result of Whitfield's 'Great Awakening'. Before sailing to Georgia he preached in Bristol churches, but on his return in 1739, he was banned from preaching in church. This forced him to preach in the open air, especially to the allegedly savage colliers of Kingswood. He invited John Wesley to join him and in 1739 they laid the first stone of their New Room in Broadmead. It was more a working building than a place of worship, to house travelling preachers and to help the poor with food and healthcare. Wesley experimented with electricity and there is an account of him setting a woman's arm on fire. They also opened a school at Kingswood to train the sons of preachers. The Countess of Huntington sponsored them and she opened a chapel in the former theatre on St Augustine's Back, now The Centre.

John Wesley became the most widely travelled person in eighteenth century England and Ireland. His congregations could reach 1,000. He established the practice of preachers travelling circuits. The class system – the precursor of microcredit – was invented to raise funds for projects such as church building. He also organised preachers to go to North America. His brother Charles and his family lived in Charles Street where he wrote many of his hymns and produced much of the movement's literature.

John Wesley was also unusual in being a high church Anglican, and he never intended to found a movement, merely to improve the existing system. He timed his services to avoid clashes with the Anglicans, and he remained on good terms with many of them. He pioneered social services like free dispensaries, and experimented with health treatments such as the use of electricity. He also helped French prisoners of war. Unfortunately he was slow to condemn the Atlantic slave trade.

Moravians

They were unusual for being pre-Reformation Protestants. The group originated in Germany and when they came to England were often associated with the Wesleys. They were very successful evangelists and travellers, who settled in most countries of the world. Their newsletters were probably the most widely read documents after the Bible.

Mary Anne Schimmelpenninck was born in Birmingham, the daughter of gunmaker Samuel Galton. Whilst on holiday in Wales as a child, she saw a Moravian funeral. It was preceded by wind instruments and some singing. The pall and mourners were all in white, with suitable scripture texts affixed such as "Blessed are the dead which die in the Lord". She claimed they called dying "going home" so they gave thanks and sang praises instead of dirges.

Unitarians

The Unitarians were important social reformers. In the USA they were second only to the Quakers in helping runaway slaves. They also campaigned on issues such as prison reform. Many members were scientists and educators, including the chemist Joseph Priestley. Dr Lant Carpenter was a respected preacher and teacher. His daughter Mary worked with him to educate the poor and helped the many homeless children, or 'Street Arabs' in Bristol. She was an important campaigner for children's rights. Her crusading writings resulted in the passage of the Youthful Offenders Act, which was referred to as 'the Magna Carta of the neglected child'. Lady Byron funded her institution at the Red Lodge, the the world's first female reformatory to help educate and train girls. It is now a city museum. Mary's elder brother William Benjamin was tutor in the household of Lord Lovelace, Byron's son-in-law. Mary was also an active abolitionist who promoted female education and suffrage. She was a successful missionary and promoter of women's rights in India. Her grave in the centre of Arnos Vale Cemetery demonstrates the respect accorded to her by the city.

Jews

In 1066 when Harding, ancestor of the Berkeleys was mayor of Bristol, he moved the Fraternity of Calendaries from Christ Church to all Hallows, now all Saints. Leland claims they founded schools for the conversion of Jews in Bristol. Probably as a result of this, in the reign of Edward I, there were few Jews in Bristol. They lived outside the town walls beside the River Frome between St John's and St Giles' gates. In 1275, Bristol became a gathering point for the region after Jews were ejected from Gloucester. But in 1290, Edward expelled all Jews from England. Jews did not return to the city until 1756, and again had to live outside the main centre. Their first synagogue was built in Temple Street. In 1759 a plot of land with a house was sold which included the Jews' burial ground. This suggests there was a community, but not a rich one. In 1786 they bought the hall of the nearly extinct Weavers' Company to convert to a synagogue. The physician and antiquarian William Barrett claimed they decorated it in "a neat and expensive manner". In 1753 a bill to naturalise Jews was strongly opposed by citizens who with the Society of Merchant Venturers signed an address to MPs.

Huguenots

The Huguenots were the best-known and by far the most successful of the many immigrant groups to the city. They fled France following the revocation by Louis XIV in 1685 of the Edict of Nantes which had allowed them freedom of worship. They came mostly from Poitou and the Biscay coast, arriving in Bristol in three waves. The first were mostly poor and in need of charity. But as there was no system to support such strangers, so they were sent on to Ireland.

Later arrivals included mariners, who found work easily, and some wealthy merchants and physicians. Rich families settled in St Stephen's parish which included the quayside and half of Queen Square. These families can be identified by their names, such as

Laroche, Daltera, Piguenet and Casamajor. Huguenot Mary Anne Peloquin was the last of her line. Her plain monument in St Stephen's church shows she left a huge legacy to charities, including her home on Queen Square to be used as a vicarage. Other families anglicised their names. – Le Roy became King, Leveret became Hare – so their histories have been lost. Eighteenth century building contractors such as Glascodine and Millerd may have been Huguenots. The Paty family may also have been members of this community. The first recorded was James Patty (or Paty) in Broadmead in the 1720s.

Some Huguenots maintained their own church until the early eighteenth century. From 1687 to 1721 they shared St Mark's, College Green with the Red Maids School. When it became the Lord Mayor's Chapel in 1722 they built a chapel in Orchard Street.

Water Supply

While the incoming tides served to clean Bristol's harbour, the River Avon's huge tidal swings meant that freshwater from upstream was intermittent. It was thus fortunate that the town was surrounded by many hills where springs could be used as sources of water. This may have been part of the attraction for the many religious orders which settled round the outskirts of the town. Each built their own conduit and provided public outlets. The antiquarian and publisher Joseph Leech claimed: "there was perhaps no city in England that from the beginning of the 13th to the end of the 16th century was so well supplied with water". Thus, of the many changes caused by The Reformation, supply of clean water was one of the most harmful, especially to the poor.

These outlets were centrally placed in their area, often within an ornate shelter. They were important street furniture and landmarks, often beside a cross, stocks, pillory and whipping post. At the Reformation, funds for their upkeep were commandeered or lost, so many pipes and reservoirs were neglected, and some failed. Queen Elizabeth I ordered the conversion of stone coffins into horse troughs, hence their modern shape. During the Commonwealth, collecting water was deemed to be work. Accordingly, an ordinance passed in 1654 decreed that all conduits should be closed and locked during divine service.

As Bristol's population grew, the dumping of human and animal waste became a problem. Down the centre of the main streets were channels or 'gouts' for waste which were flushed out when it rained. But these were allegedly damaged by wheeled vehicles. In Bristol, such vehicles were banned and replaced with sledges within the city. Settlements whose names ended in 'bourne' had streams down their main streets to provide household water, but in the dry summer months, locals relied on wells. This was also the pattern in Cheltenham and Salisbury till the channels became polluted and were filled in during the 19th century.

Leech claimed the pipes were only for the clerics who built them, showing they were driven by self-interest. But the religious houses also cared for the poor and the sick. Public water supplies were free, while wealthy households were charged for a branch to their homes which was called 'a feather'. Maps of the supply looked like feathers, and the pipes were often the width of a feather. Persons helping themselves to access were condemned for 'feathering their nests'.

All Saints' Pipe was built by the Grey Friars from a bubbling well in the priory garden on Kingsdown. It supplied St James' Priory, then St Bartholomew's Hospital at the base of Christmas Steps before running along Lewin's Mead and up Broad Street. It ended at an ornate castellette, a castle-like shelter on All Saints' church in Corn Street. It seems to have supplied the Corn Exchange and the adjoining coffee house when they were built in the 1740s.

When John Leland dined at the Carmelite friary, he described St John's Conduit to be the town's finest. The friars built a conduit from an abundant spring on Brandon Hill for their own use and provided a branch to St John's on the Wall. In 1376 a plumber was paid £10 p.a. for life to maintain the supply to All Saints' and St John's conduits from the friary cistern. His wages were paid by the rents from two houses on Bristol Bridge. The lead pipes were intended to last forever.

Temple Pipe arose in a cavern on the bank of the Avon at Totterdown. Lord Knowle granted it to the Knights of St John, successors to the Templars. It seems to have been lost or fallen into disrepair at the Reformation, as Barratt claims it was built in 1561 and two tenements donated to pay for its repairs, and large sums spent on maintaining it, possibly due to its closeness to the river. A large freestone reservoir was 125 yards from the source, where more springs added to the flow. He claimed it was a huge 10 to 20 feet high in places. It ended at a public sheltered cistern near Temple gate, near Lord Knowle's house in 1366, and supplied the Augustinian brothers near Temple gate. It later ended at the Neptune statue and outlet on Temple Street. Like St Mary Redcliffe's pipe, its route was confirmed with an annual walk and a feast by church officers. After the Reformation it was funded by rents from Temple fair. But when a publican complained of the fair's beer tents damaging his business, the event was abolished. The pipe's outlet is now lost.

Redcliffe Pipe was built by Robert de Berkeley from his Huge — or Ruge — well at Knowle. Leyland claimed its outlet had a castellette against the church wall, beside the parish stocks. It also supplied nearby St John's Hospital.

St Thomas's parish was supplied by a well, paid for by a parishioner. But in 1566 the Redcliffe Pipe was redirected to it from St John's Hospital after the latter closed and the 2 churches shared the costs of repairing the pipe. The rent was 12 pence p.a. In 1570 Elizabeth I granted the mayor permission for a Thursday market in St Thomas Street. Tolls from the sale of wool, cattle etc. were to fund the local almshouse. But the conduit had to move to make way for this. The remains of the outlet is against the former Wool Hall on St Thomas St.

Quay Pipe arose at Ashley Down from two boiling wells. It was conveyed to the city via Newfoundland Road and Haymarket. Few records survive beyond reports of the corporation paying for dead cats to be removed from its source. Its outlet was on the quay near St Stephen's church. Leech claimed it was the city's finest, and the only one not built by monks. By the 18th century it was the main source of fresh water for overseas shipping and for fighting fires when the tide was out. In 1717 the fish market was nearby so it helped maintain standards of hygiene there. A plaque on the quay claims that by 1870 it was fed by St John's Conduit. The pipes have no statutory protection, so this change may have been caused by builders along the route.

St Peter's Pump and St Edith's Well were often used interchangeably, so it is hard to be clear whether they were separate. The term pump rather than well suggests St Peter's took over the water source when the water pressure, hence supply fell. Whatever the name, it was in the Saxon town so may have been the oldest man-made water sources. St Edith was an ancient Saxon saint, a contemporary of the better known St Werburgh. The first mention of her well was as a landmark in a 14th century will. When Castle Park was laid out in 1998, the site of St Edith's Well was to be a feature. But it is now only a depression in the line of trees near the park's Wine Street entrance.

In 1546 the founder of the city grammar school, Nicholas Thorne, left funds to repair St Peter's conduit house, as well as the Pithay Well and St Peter's Pump. In 1586 Ralph Dole left the rent of 1 pound from a tenement on Mary Port Street to keep the pump in repair. In 1660 the freemason Henry Hoare restored St Peter's Pump for the visit of Charles II. In 1661 he was paid to set up a picture (or possibly a bust) at the pump. In 1680 stones were installed to protect the pump from drays, and stocks were placed against its wall. But claims were made that it could be pumped dry when the tide was out. As the pump was in the area being renovated to help pay for the rebuilding of Bristol Bridge, it seems its upkeep became their responsibility. In 1766 they held a meeting at which they decided to remove St Peter's Cross and Pump immediately. It was to be replaced with a new pump on St Peter's Street which would be supplied with a feather from the well. Though not mentioned, this suggests it was an obstruction to traffic. The banker Henry Hoare had already installed the city's High Cross at his grand estate at Stourhead, so he offered to take down the structure on condition there was no charge for the stones. This is widely seen as an act of antiquary, but he was also preserving the work of his ancestor. Thomas Paty was the surveyor for finishing the bridge and its approaches, so he also arranged for its relocation. Like all the other water pipes which remained, it was closed as a health hazard in 1887.

As the city expanded, many of the pipes wore out or were damaged or destroyed by building works. The survivors became redundant when the city converted to a mains water supply. But in World War II, bombs damaged the main pipe from Bedminster. In September 1941, holes were dug in the middle of Park Street to help fire fighting. The Evening Post asked "what would the old friars have thought of their water supply having been used to encounter the fire-raising of a so-called Christian nation warring against another after 600 years of progress?"

The various water supplies were not merely a system of lead or elm pipes. Underground reservoirs maintained water pressure. As they were built and maintained by the various religious houses, they were all sold to the city by Henry VIII at the dissolution of the monasteries. The Carmelite system was a state of the art water supply which included tunnels for maintenance. There were purification and settling tanks filled with iron stone to create chaotic flow which caused the silt to settle out. This system was also used at Waltham Abbey. The Carmelites were linked to the universities so their engineering knowledge was cutting edge. Because these systems have no statutory protection, few people are aware of them. They are probably the source of the many rumours of slave tunnels and cellars beneath the city.

About a mile downstream on the Avon is the remains of the Hotwells spring and the spa that grew around it. The water was described by William of Worcestre as being "milk warm", but he made no claims of any healing properties. Sailors filled barrels with it as they embarked on long journeys. Perhaps it was cleaner than any of the city's water or the minerals may have kept it fresh on such voyages.

The visit of Catherine of Braganza, wife of Charles II, in 1677 seems to have begun its rise in popularity and the commercial exploitation of the site. In 1695 the Merchant Venturers offered a 99 year lease on condition the tenants built a pump room and other facilities. The lease included land from the high-water mark to the top of the cliffs, i.e., the Downs, and the public still had free access to the well at low tide.

From 1754 a daily coach ran between Bristol and Bath for 10 shillings and 6 pence, with an extra fare of 1 shilling and 6 pence to Hotwells. But the resort's success was limited by its lack of lodgings. The first visitors stayed at College Green near the cathedral. The spa's popularity was helped by the rising export trade of its water in Bristol Blue bottles and in barrels. By 1752 it was shipped along the British coast as far as Glasgow and Plymouth, and to Ireland, the West Indies, Northern Europe and Africa. The water was claimed to be beneficial for a wide range of complaints. William Beckford was said to have been cured of diabetes. The spa became almost as popular as Bath. But the site of the spring's outlet below the high-tide mark needed to be walled in, so was expensive to maintain. The Merchant Venturers kept raising the rents, so by 1785 there were no takers. It went into decline and the Venturers were forced to pay for improvements. As in Bath, this decline was blamed on the Napoleonic Wars, and reflected in the wider city because Bristol had many unfinished and unsellable streets and terraces. But the real reason was that George III and his court had made Cheltenham the resort of choice. At the end of the French Wars, Europe opened up to tourists and Hotwells became known as a morgue. It mostly catered for victims of TB, many of whom sought help too late. Claims were made that the same people who kept the lodgings at Hotwells also arranged for funerals.

Visitors to the spa often walked or rode on the Downs, so lodging houses were built near the country church of Clifton. When Poet Laureate Robert Southey visited, he claimed the village of Clifton had once been the most beautiful in England, but had become the finest suburb. He described the Avon Gorge as magnificent but lacking clean water. He complained of the narrow path from the village to the gorge, and of the quarrying on Clifton and Durdham Downs. The explosions often sent rocks into the air, which added some drama to the walks, but could also cause injuries. He wrote: "The people of Bristol seem to sell everything that can be sold!"

Throughout the spa's history, local people claimed the right to free access to the spring. Early in the 20th century a grotto was built against the cliff with an ornate cast iron pump and an attendant. It was closed in 1939 and in 1969 the pump was moved to the city's museum.

In 1798 John Nott M.D. discovered a spring on the heights. An attorney dug a 250 foot deep well to reach the water, which was raised by a fire engine. He built a pump room, but his timing was bad, so he put it up for sale. Between 1816 and 1820 the fledgling company of J Schweppe & Co was selling soda water made here.

Opposite the Hotwells was the Scarlet Spring. William of Worcester wrote of it providing water for ships embarking on long voyages. From 1676 it drove a lead mill owned by Viscount Grandison. Annalist John Latimer claimed these were the 'cupeloes', a term associated with metal smelting on the Avon, recorded at the bottom of Nightingale Valley. In 1756 John Pitman was seeking support for lead smelting. But complaints were made at the spa about the clouds of smoke and by 1761 of a white substance on vegetation and houses, and there were reports of the mill's workmen becoming sick. The building was converted to a cotton mill, then a log mill before burning down in 1831. The logs were a species of tropical wood which were ground to produce dye for cloth making. The water still gushes from the bank after passing beneath the cycle and walking trail to Pill via a culvert.

Charities

John Whitson was a successful merchant and civic leader, and like the now-infamous Edward Colston, he had no legitimate sons to inherit his wealth. In his 1627 will he left most of his wealth to Bristol Corporation as executor to fund his chosen charities. The bulk of it was to found the city's first girls' school, whose pupils, the Red Maids, wore a red dress under a white apron. But following Whitson's death in 1629 his heirs who he had not trusted to manage the great wealth challenged his will so the funds were not released till 1634. It paid for 40 daughters of infirm or deceased freemen to be educated, trained and apprenticed to a mistress for 8 to 10 years. Their house was near the boys' school, Queen Elizabeth Hospital. Both schools worshipped at St Marks opposite the Cathedral on College Green and continue their connections. The school's arms are those of the Spanish Company, of which Whitson had been a member.

On 10 September, 1816, Richard Reynolds died at Cheltenham. He was possibly Bristol's greatest philanthropist. His funeral at the Quakers Friars burial ground attracted huge numbers of citizens, many of whom had benefited from his generosity. He was born in Bristol and apprenticed to William Fry, then worked with Abraham Darby II whose daughter he married. He spent most of his life making vast sums from managing and improving the iron furnaces at Coalbrookdale, while pioneering workers' welfare. He also improved the funding of almshouses when they greatly needed support during the Napoleonic Wars. When he retired, he returned to Bristol and his almoners sought out deserving causes. He is thought to have given £300,000 to charity, including funding an extension to the Bristol Royal Infirmary, plus unknown amounts that he gave away anonymously.

Another great benefactor to the city was Samuel Morley whose statue survives on The Centre. He was one of the great Victorian industrialist politicians. He served as a Liberal MP for Nottingham before moving to Bristol where he was MP from 1868 to 1885. He was involved in several violent elections, and was twice injured by mobs. For many years he dispersed £20-30,000 each year for "pious and philanthropic objects", including the campaign for higher education. He had a long and distinguished career in charity and public service and was commemorated by a statue which is included in walk no. 6, 'God's Many Houses', plus a chapel, now demolished. The plinth quotes him: "I believe that the power of England is to be reckoned not by her wealth or armies but by the purity and virtue of the great mass of her population."

Commerce

Bristol is unusual in never having been a county town, i.e., a centre for local agriculture. But it was the only major port between the Midlands and Bridgwater. Its trade always faced west, to Wales and Ireland. Until the mid-19th century, it was the economic centre for southern Wales and Ireland, so it attracted many immigrants. In times of trouble and/or food shortages this stretched the finite capacities of local charities and the authorities to their limits.

Bristol's first charter dates from 1155. It granted her citizens toll-free passage through the king's dominions of England, Wales and Normandy. It also reconfirmed established liberties. Thus Bristol has the longest and best-documented history of rights outside of London. Her citizens were independent of local lords, could marry freely and build between the town walls and the riverside. Bristol expanded to become a major trading port, especially with Ireland. A few years later a similar document granted the inhabitants "in the marsh by Bristol Bridge" permission to found a chapel of ease for the region of Bedminster. This is the first mention of what became St Mary Redcliffe. Its main door faces north towards the town, showing the location of most of its parishioners.

In 1171 a further charter effectively made Dublin effectively a trading colony of Bristol. Camden claimed that an English colony was 'transplanted' from Bristol to Dublin, as it was given to them by Henry II with the same freedoms and liberties as Bristol. It flourished from that date. This was possibly to ensure the town's loyalty to the English Crown. Waterford and Limerick were soon granted similar rights. In 1188 another of her charters described Bristol as a borough, granting her merchants free passage throughout the kingdom. This was a huge gain, as they did not have to pay tolls at gates or customs dues at ports. When Charles I issued trade monopolies to his court favourites, Bristol merchants disputed them as a breach of their rights. Bristol's great annual fairs had for centuries been dominated by the wool trade. Bristol's new rights forced merchants to buy their cloth only at the fairs to avoid competition with local shopkeepers.

Bristol's trade was always diverse. Merchants exported a wide range of goods such as wool, hides, iron, lead, fish, live animals, wool and cloth. The town established its own guilds. Religious guilds were to support the church. Trade guilds provided welfare for their members.They evolved into the various trade guilds to train, support and protect the practitioners of their professions. This was especially important when merchants established centres or 'factories' abroad. They were often treated as aliens so had to support each other and were often at risk of eviction, especially when wars broke out. They enforced high standards of quality and honesty, as they would be forced to make good any debts of their colleagues, which ensured their customers that they were trustworthy.

By the end of the 12th century, it seems the largest guild was that of soap makers. Cotswolds wool was exchanged in Iberia for olive oil, generating huge profits for both sides. By 1300 Bristol's guild of weavers was established, after being granted their own chapel in Temple church. With allied trades such as tuckers and dyers, the region became a major industrial area. Woollen cloth became the region's major export, and its merchants became the biggest and most powerful group in the town. By c.1400 an estimated 1,500 people were employed in cloth-related trades. They exported cloth to the Low Countries, though they never equalled volumes of England's better-placed the eastern ports.

Bristol became a major gathering point for wool from Gloucestershire, especially the Cotswolds, and from South Wales. The trade needed to be organised via justices and customs, so the 'staple' was introduced. This was a monopoly clearing house to organise the trade and ensure the high quality of goods and honest commerce.

By 1344 the town's records note 17 professions were large enough to form guilds. As well as providing mutual support and organising training via apprenticeships, they ensured high standards for goods. The Fraternity of St John the Baptist was founded in 1392. From its chapel in St Ewen's, it grew to become the Merchant Taylors' Society.

Britain remained predominantly rural until the 19th century. Disease kept down the populations of cities, so young country people acted as healthy immigrants. Medieval Bristol was large by English standards, but still much smaller than London. The capital was the only city which compared with European centres, especially the city states of Italy and the Low Countries. Bristol's medieval trade was mainly local. But ships sailing to Europe also transported pilgrims to destinations such as Santiago de Compostella and the Holy Land.

William Canynge the younger was the most famous merchant of that period. In the 1460s he owned nine ships, probably built by himself, which employed eight hundred men plus a further one hundred land-based workmen. He is often credited with funding the rebuilding of St Mary Redcliffe, but he only contributed to this. He founded two chantries, including one housed in the churchyard.

For centuries, Bristol's wool trade dominated the town, but it peaked in the 1440s. By 1500 the town specialised in red cloth, made from local flowers and was the colour of its aldermen's robes. This echoed the local specialities of other cities, like Lincoln Green and Coventry Blue. In the early fourteenth century the town also traded in pelts, including those of squirrel and cats. Icelandic cod and stockfish were exchanged in Calais, Bordeaux and Gascony. When the church declared Fridays should be meat-free, this was a boon to local fisheries. Dried and salted fish provided long-life high protein food to supplement winter stores, for long distance journeys and for armies, so there was a huge market for it. Bristol imported Spanish wine and dried fruit, olive oil for soapmakers, and iron for Bristol smelters. In 1466 an important trade treaty was signed between Bristol and Castille but this ended with the Armada. This was widely seen as a territorial invasion, but was an attempt to reclaim these islands for the Church of Rome, so was a religious crusade. The fleet failed largely due to bad weather, so was widely seen by the English that God had been on their side, so further strengthened the grounds for Protestantism.

By 1449 the number of guilds had risen to 26, about a third of which were involved in the cloth trade. Strangely for a maritime town, the Mariners' Guild was not formed until 1445. They caught fish which they salted and sold. Possibly mariners were reluctant to organise because they were secretive about the routes they sailed to catch the best fish.

Following the Reformation, guilds lost their religious roles but some continued as organisations dedicated to supporting and expanding their various trades. In 1550 the Fellowship of Merchants, like the earlier Guild of Merchants, met in Spicers' Hall on Welsh

Back. The Bakers' Guild met in the former Dominican church in what is now the Quakers' Friars area of the Merchant Quarter.

The city was struck by one of its worst outbreaks of plague in 1575–6, with over 2,000 dead, including 4 former mayors. This seems to have inspired a shift towards mechanisation, as had followed the Black Death when spectacles, compasses and the printing press were invented. Heavy industries such as metal smelting increased in the region, which polluted the rivers, and drove cloth making to the Cotswold valleys and their clean water. Bristol maintained its role in exporting the finished cloth. Squatters settled in the former Royal Chase of Kingswood to dig coal, fuelling the expansion of the city's industries. Early attempts were made in the castle at brass making, encouraged by the government because brass cannons were less likely to explode than those of brittle iron. Brass wire was also used for pin-making, with the industry employing poor children in Bristol and Gloucestershire.

The number of soap makers in the city peaked at 27, but this was down to eleven by the early 17th century. The Armada caused problems with olive oil supplies, so locals shifted to the use of 'trane', i.e., seal or whale oil, used to oil combs to untangle raw wool. But the stench drove them back to Spanish supplies when peace was declared in 1610. The soap makers built a new hall, then another in 1633. However, Bristol's annual output was limited to six hundred tons by the Stuarts' practice of issuing licences to court favourites. The royals helped fund their court by the sale of these trade monopolies, but the practice resulted in campaigns at court to open up the affected trades. This abuse of monopolies was a major factor in Bristol's support for the Parliamentary cause when the Civil War broke out.

Tobacco

Virginia tobacco was introduced to the West Country by Raleigh in 1586. However, tobacco remained generally unpopular until the better-tasting West Indian variety replaced the local cultivar to be grown and exported from Virginia. Richard Fletcher was bishop of Worcester who died suddenly of "immoderate use of tobacco" in June

1596, so there may have been genuine concern of its dangers, possibly from nicotine poisoning.

But James I objected to smoking and published his 'Counterblast To Tobacco' in 1604. Claims have been made that he objected to the smoke as a health risk or to its suggested links with the use of incense in the Catholic Church. It was due to customs dues, paid by imports only. But the weed's popularity grew, and in 1620 the king granted a monopoly to London merchants. This was opposed by Gloucester growers, especially around Winchcombe, where unemployment and crime were rising. Pepys wrote that the Life Guard were sent to destroy the crop, wrongly claiming the locals had always grown it. A 1655 tract by 'Henry the Hangman' bemoaned the fall in his employment as the poor were no longer driven to sheep stealing and other capital crimes to survive. Locals supported the growing of the crop as it provided much needed work, so keeping down poor rates and crime. Magistrates often failed to punish those who flouted the ban as they were happy to pocket the rents.

In the 1630s Bristol and other western ports were given occasional import licences. The extent of lawbreaking probably made the monopoly unenforceable. Local tobacco pipe makers breached yet another London monopoly.

Starch makers of Bristol and Norwich also complained of their trade being restricted by London monopolies.

As settlement in the Americas expanded, the axis of maritime trade tilted towards the western ports, especially Bristol. Martin Pring was a member of the Merchant Venturers and in 1603 the society funded him to explore the region later settled by the Pilgrim Fathers. He produced detailed maps and planted crops to test their viability.

But the city played only a marginal role in early investment in the colonies, probably as it was still on its knees after the Civil War. Huge tracts of land in North America were sold to London companies expecting huge profits. Bristol became a major departure port for the New World, with 10,000 people sailing to North America between 1654 and 1685. Half went to Virginia as indentured servants. From the late 17th century, Virginian 'argosies' arrived during July and

August. Bristol's summer fair expanded into a celebration of the huge wealth they brought, and of the ships' crews being reunited with their families. Pepys saw the launch of The Edgar on his visit to the 1668 fair. By the 1670s Norwich had become England's second city, but Bristol was the second port.

Civil War

At the outbreak of the seventeenth century Civil War, Bristol was seen by both sides as the major prize after London. It was crucial to hold the West and its wealth, so the city came close to becoming the nation's second capital. The citizens had long endured the king's extortions and the abuse of trade and industries by his favourites. But this was balanced by the traditional rivalry with the eastern ports which were also the Parliamentary heartlands, home to religious fanaticism. The situation was complicated and volatile.

Bristolians' priority was always the protection of their city as continuity in trade prevented them starving. Many swapped allegiance to suit the circumstances, leading to later accusations of opportunism. In 1642, in the early stages of the war, Bristol was held by Parliament. But the city's defence was hampered by its spread beyond the old walls. People could not retreat to the safety of the castle. Extensive fortifications were needed to link 3 high points and surround the outlying region. Guns were placed on the Marsh to defend the river.

By the following year, Prince Rupert held most of the West Country. This increased Bristol's importance, both symbolically and for plundering its wealth. A plot to admit Royalists through the Frome Gate was thwarted and the two leaders were executed, becoming martyrs. The outer walls at the top of what is now Park Street were breached by Colonel Washington, ancestor to the future American president. In the final defence, Dorothy Hazard and a group of women blocked Frome Gate with wool sacks. But two regiments led by Colonel Essex were admitted by Mrs Rogers and Mrs Vikris.

By 27 July 1643 Royalists held Bristol, removing the final Parliamentary outpost in the West. There was talk of the royal court moving there, which would have caused further depredations and harm to what remained of the local economy. Bristol lost merchant ships to Dunkirkers and Algerian pirates as well as Puritans. Rupert ordered many houses outside the city walls to be swept away to improve security. Others were burnt or damaged by his soldiers, especially in Bedminster to the south, where the parish church was burnt down. Bristol became the last West Country centre to fall to Parliament, and Prince Rupert departed on 10 September 1645. He had plundered the city, leaving the starving inhabitants looking more like prisoners than citizens.

Not all the clergy lost their livings, and the cathedral was largely undamaged, but the greatest outrage was the sale of the Bishop's Palace. The lead was stripped from the roof while the bishop's wife was in labour; she died, and was soon followed by her husband. Cromwell ordered the departure of the garrison and for the castle to be 'slighted' to remove its military capacity. Justices passed regulations for the removal and sale of its Caen stone facing. The city chamberlain was granted most of the Military House. With the gardens, it was later owned by Thomas Goldney, the Quaker grocer. He was the main investor in Woodes Rogers' voyage and his descendant built the Clifton mansion. The rest went to a minister and to the cathedral.

Post-War Recovery

John Evelyn visited the city in 1654 and saw a sugar refinery where eggs were fried for him in the furnace. He described the castle as being "of no concernment". Castle Street had already replaced the chaotic 'Alsatia' of the Precincts and provided a proper route between Old Market and the centre. New houses soon provided rents to help the city's recovery. The castle was finally demolished in 1657. Local builders were granted contracts to develop the region, recycling the castle stone for building and grinding it up for mortar and roads. Millerd's map of 1673 shows Newgate was the only surviving gate, used as the debtors' prison. Though faced with Bath Stone, it was described by eighteenth century reformer John Howard as "white without and black within". The dungeon for the poorest prisoners was infamous for its dark, filthy condition.

By 1686 the corporation's debts were a massive £16,000. More of the Castle Precincts were sold, road cleaning and repairs were stopped, and even fur trimmings were removed from official robes.

By 1670 the tobacco trade had risen to comprise half the city's imports. Bristol was also famous for its shipbuilding, but settlement in the nearby woodland, especially of coal miners in Kingswood, caused a shortage of large timbers. Masts had to be imported from the Forest of Dean. Bristol built mostly small merchantmen. Other ships were built at Lydney on the River Wye, then fitted out in Bristol, though the city was unable to make large anchors.

After the Civil War, the old town walls were no longer needed for defence. They remained to collect tolls until they were removed for causing an obstruction to traffic. The rich moved to the healthy air and space of Kingsdown and Clifton, leaving the old city to continue its decline. Buildings on Bristol Bridge had encroached onto the roadway as traffic increased. The bridge was rebuilt in the 1760s, and the costs were to be recouped by the sale of properties on the new Bridge Street. This was the city's first attempt at emulating the success of Bath's town planning. The intention was to replace the medieval Worshipful Street. This included the Butchers' Shambles which became redundant when St Nicholas' Markets were built in the 1740s. While the street initially failed to attract investors, it eventually became the region's first terrace of uniform stone housing. It improved access to the bridge, and helped to pay off the debts of the bridge's construction.

Bristol in the 18th century was overshadowed by its more genteel neighbour of Bath. But comparisons between the two are often unfair, as Bristol was a working city and a port, not a resort. Annalist John Latimer claimed at the start of the century the average citizen was "as illiterate as the back of a tombstone". While records show that some of the city's leaders were unable to sign their names, this seems unfair and probably inaccurate overall. People in trade needed to keep accounts, keep track of stock, borrow or lend money, to pay rates and taxes, so it seems more likely they were functionally literate. Like travellers abroad, they learnt what they needed to get by. This is why the benefactions of Edward Colston and other rich merchants made such a huge impact. They often left funds to clothe and educate the sons and daughters of poor or orphaned freemen. And their efforts worked. Possibly inspired by Colston, or reflecting the economic recovery of the time, by the 1730s the city had some fine teachers. As the century progressed private academies were established, with several on St Michael's Hill. By the 1770s the private Library Society was flourishing.

When Daniel Defoe visited in the 1720s he noted the overcrowded Tolzey where taxes were paid and the council met. He wrote of the well-populated hinterland which promised a ready market for imports. Bristol was also a large port and market, a base for transhipping coastal products for distribution inland. It was a major international port, and its huge tidal swings powered many mills on the Avon and Trim Mills where the Malago joined it.

Polite Society

Funding for schools was not enough to create what became established as polite society in such a crowded working port. The Theatre Royal and the library were both in King Street. They were convenient for the affluent residents of Queen Square and Princes Street. Both were supported by a wide range of local society, even including some Quakers, though by then many were less pious than their radical forebears.

Geography also played a role. The Hotwells' Spring became a popular Spa. It was popularised by the day trip from Bath of Queen Henrietta Maria on 20 July 1677. By 1695 a house had been built and the spring enclosed to protect it from the tides. Spa visitors often combined the medicinal water with visits to the surrounding countryside. They could cross the Avon to Long Ashton and Leigh Woods, and climb the rocks up to the Downs for spectacular views. The dramatic scenery also attracted artists such as Francis Danby. Nearby St Vincents Rock also had a spring. It attracted geologists in search of a type of spar called Bristol Stones. William of Worcestre visited it in 1480. He described the rock and a chapel of 9 yards by 3 or 6.

Thomas Chatterton is now mostly known for his fraudulent poetry and unfortunate end. But his early rambles in the countryside, especially to the spectacular Avon Gorge, inspired him to write romantic poetry. Thus he was a forerunner of the Romantic poets Southey and Coleridge.

Like Bath, the spa at Hotwells attracted physicians and scientists. They hoped to profit from invalids and to investigate treatments. Dr Thomas Beddoes left his post of reader in chemistry at Oxford in 1792 to allow his independent research to be funded by wealthy patients. He did not believe in the benefits of the local waters, being more interested in the study and medicinal benefits of gases. This led to such strange experiments as having patients share a room with a cow as protection against smallpox. He found support among the wealthy visitors to the spa and established his Pneumatic Institute at Hotwells for which James Watt provided equipment. Lack of space led to lodgings being built on the heights of Clifton, and Beddoes stayed at Rodney Place in 1792-3. His home became an important centre for progressive society. In 1799 John and Josiah Wedgwood, sons of the potter Josiah were staying at Clifton as his patients. Josiah the elder was a member of the famous Lunar Society, a group of friends in the Midlands who met for dinner and to share ideas on science and the arts between 1765 and 1813. Beddoes' home became the venue for a local version of the group.

Wordsworth was living at Westbury-on-Trym and also sought treatment from Beddoes. The young Humphrey Davy worked at the institute. Davy knew the polymath R. L. Edgeworth and other Lunar Men who had stayed at his mother's lodging house in Cornwall when they were seeking sources of clay for their pottery. Edgeworth provided financial support for the institute. His eldest daughter, Anna Maria, married Beddoes. Another daughter, Maria, worked with her father to promote agricultural improvements on their Irish estate, and on improving education for children. She made more from her novels than Austen or Scott and inspired the latter to write the Waverley novels. R.L. Edgeworth was a close friend of Thomas Day whose poetry condemned slavery. They obtained two young women from a workhouse to be trained to become Day's perfect wife. Maria visited a slave ship in the port, so this same society was also involved in abolition of the slave trade.

Benjamin Donn, later Donne, produced some of the finest maps of Bristol, and worked as a surveyor and teacher of maths and navigation. He became the city librarian, ran a mathematical academy at the library, published books and gave public lectures on geometry and navigation. He later became master of mathematics to the king and his geometric models were praised by Beddoes and the Edgeworths. In this way, as the port of Bristol declined, a centre of enlightenment thinking established itself. Clifton College was founded, based on Rugby. There were also many local societies, many of which were faith based, and are described in several of the walks.

INSTRUCTIONS FOR WALKS

The original collection was published as single stand-alone sheets. This was to encourage users to follow single walks or to run several together. This allowed the 13 walks to expand to provide a much larger selection. This is still encouraged. Possible combinations are as follows:

Walks 1 & 2 cover the area of Castle Park.

Walks 3 & 4 cover streets of the old city, and can be done in sequence. They can also be combined with walks 1 and 2.

Walks 5, 6 & 7, are longer, and follow specific themes, so can stand alone.

Walk 8 can be followed by either 9 or 10. It starts near Castle Park, so can also follow 1 & 2.

Walk 10 can be followed by 11

The maps have been drawn to fit the page, and serve their purpose in conjunction with the text. For more detail, accurate maps of the area can be found online or in city guides.

Many walks pass attractions and venues. Please check their websites for opening times if you wish to visit.

Most walks begin and end within reach of public transport. Please check relevant websites for details. This is especially important in relation to The Cut, parts of which are in a dangerous state, so may still be closed to pedestrians.

All details are accurate at the time of publication. If any errors are found, please contact the author who will list them on her website and if necessary, amend any future editions.

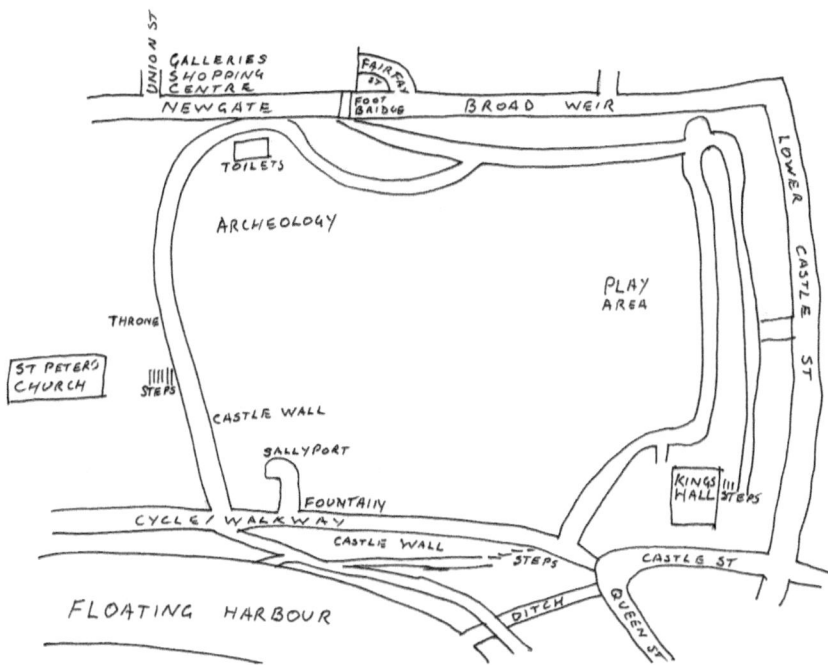

ONE

Round the Castle

Start: Entrance to Castle Park, opposite The Galleries shopping centre

End: The walk is circular

Length: Approx. 1 km/ 0.75 miles

Route: Entirely in public park. Several gentle slopes, two small flights of steps

Public Transport: Any buses to city centre/Broadmead/Old Market

PREAMBLE

The earliest evidence of settlement of this area comes from Saxon coins issued by Cnut. They show the site was important enough to be classified as a burgh which was minting its own coins by about 1020 AD. The Domesday Book indicates it was a flourishing settlement in the 11th century. It was built to protect trade and collect the king's taxes. It was well sited above the River Avon which was fordable at low tide. The River Frome or Froom flowed round its base from the east, close to the line of modern Baldwin Street. This river drove the mill which ground corn for the castle, making it the town"s oldest industrial site. The corporation bought the mill for demolition in 1824. Millerd's map of 1674 shows the ducking stool on its pond to punish scolding women and market fraudsters. Spectators could view punishments from an adjoining pub.

Bristol's name is said to be Saxon for 'the place of the bridge', but this could mean an embankment or ford. It probably began as a place for travellers to cross the river at low tide. However, many places have bridges but are not named after them. The Frome is now mostly covered over in the city centre. It once had 7 bridges crossing it.

The first town seal dates from 1359 when Edward III replaced the original English arms. It has an accurate image of the castle, with one turret higher than the others. The ship was initially shown entering the castle's watergate, but the design soon changed to show it leaving, suggesting a shift from it being a place of shelter to a base for trade. With fish and eels in the water, it was vividly realistic, and the ship's design evolved to show improvements over time.

By 1000 AD Bristol had a mint and a market cross, so was a secure commercial centre in Saxon times. Archaeological remnants of leather and worked metal survive from this time. The Domesday Book lists a church but fails to provide a name. It was probably 1 of the 3 at the Saxon crossroads, now the junction of High, Wine, Broad and Corn Streets. Thus it could have been All Saints/Holy Trinity, Christ Church, St Ewens, or St Werburgh's which was on the corner of Small and Corn Streets. St Mary-le-Port's name dates from before a permanent bridge crossed the Avon, and ships moored on the sloping muddy bank from the church to the river. In the 14th century it was St Mary of Foro, and wealthy merchants' houses were built on Worshipful Street where ships unloaded to their basements. When the port moved downstream after the Civil War, these houses decayed and became the butchers' shambles. In the 15th century the church was named St Mary-of-the-Market as it was paid to allow pigs and sheep to graze before being slaughtered.

St Peter's was part of the manor of Barton Regius. It served as an intermediary between the castle and the town, as Peter held the keys to heaven. When Cromwell ordered the locals to 'slight' the castle, they allegedly demolished it with great speed, recycling the stone for new homes and business premises. In 1880 a well on Castle Green adjoining the former keep was found which contained stone cannon balls. They included some for the Cannon Royal, the largest of the 17th century siege guns.

Near The Galleries shopping centre, which dates from the 1980s, was the Newgate entrance to the castle. For many years it served as the debtors' prison. Though faced with fine freestone in the 18th century, the prison reformer John Howard described it as "white without and black within". Many died of disease there, especially in the filthy debtors' dungeon.

From Saxon times the largest markets were held at or near the main crossroads. But by the early 18th century they were an obstruction to the increasing traffic, so attempts were made to move commerce indoors. John Wood of Bath built the Corn Exchange, and the markets were built behind it by locals.

In the 1770s, Union Street — named after the union with Scotland

— was laid out to improve transport between St James' parish and the city centre markets. It involved building a new stone bridge over the From and a new market was intended to reduce congestion in Corn Street. But it was never popular.

From the late 19th century until the Blitz, the old castle region was the main shopping area. There were pool halls, pubs, shops and even a vegetarian restaurant. The area also had two of the most modern cinemas of the period. The Regent had ceiling tiles by Walter Yoxall who was responsible for Everard's Printing Works on Broad Street. The city's first police station was on Wine Street before it moved to Bridewell. For 250 years, the precinct was as famous for promenading as for shopping. Locals caught trams into the bustling centre on Saturday nights. Street hawkers, barrel organs, performing lions, boxing matches, waxworks, escapologists and jugglers performed. Shops stayed open late to sell off their perishable goods. This allowed low income families to get their Sunday roasts at big discounts.

At the far end was Castle Street Mixed School, established in 1887, which was famous for producing rugby players. It had a swimming pool in the basement and a playground on the roof. After the Blitz, the fairground became the Marks & Spencers' store. For many years the council wanted to modernise the area, and many chain stores were eager to have sites there. The ancient wooden buildings were decaying, so even before the bombs, there was at high risk of fires. The authorities saw the Blitz damage as a chance to develop the region. The inner city was largely depopulated, with many old buildings being demolished as suburban estates were built.

In the 1970s local artists installed pieces of site-specific sculpture. This pioneering initiative was to encourage people to visit the area. Sir Hugh Casson provided detailed proposals to move the bombed museum on Park Street and establish a cultural centre. But after much debate the scheme was diluted to establish Castle Park in 1978. When The Galleries shopping centre was being built, the area was used as a carpark in return for funding the park.

With support from several other sponsors, the area was landscaped, and the present scheme was opened in 1992 with a grand ceremony. The castle-themed children's playground has gone, but the site-specific sculptures survive, and new information boards have recently been installed. In 2006 the council planned to build on Castle Park and 'develop' it to fund basic maintenance. A public campaign involving this author and The Evening Post stopped this plan. Arguments continue over the park's fate, because arguing is what the modern city is famous for.

THE AMBLE
Begin at the entrance to Castle Park, opposite Union Street.

The large bronze sculpture is 'Line From Within' by Ann Christopher. It represents the New Gate to the castle. It is on loan to the park from the Royal West of England Academy which commissioned it.

Veer left to see the large white sculpture, 'The Empty Throne', by Rachel Fenner which is set into a hedge to the north of the ruins of St Peter's church.

It is carved from Normandy sandstone, which was used to face the castle. It represents the long-absent Norman conquerors. The importation of stone seems to make little sense, as it is heavy and the region had plenty of its own stone at Dundry which was later used for the Cathedral and as far away as Strata Florida in mid Wales. Much of the town was built of local stone though its colours were dark and uneven. It was probably used for ballast as Bristol exported a lot of wool and grain to Europe. The statue has recently been damaged.

Retrace your steps towards St Peter's church. Turn left to follow the water feature which ends with a water maze.

'Beside the Still Waters' is by Peter Randall Page and the city engineers' department. Continue down some steps at the far end and turn right towards the water. On your left is a brick wall emerging from a bank of earth, part of the old castle wall.

Turn left at the bicycle path to see a large bronze and ceramic sculpture by Kate Malone which is untitled.

It shows images including the ship sailing out of the castle gate based on the city's coat of arms. It is one of a series of drinking fountains placed along the Bristol to Bath Cycleway. The bricks round the base show aspects of Bristol's history illustrated by local schoolchildren.

A short path to your left leads to a gate in the side of the hill.

This was the castle's 'sallyport'. It allowed soldiers to leave the castle during sieges, especially if enemies were trying to dig under the walls.

Retrace your steps past the drinking fountain. Turn left down the path to the waterside, taking care to avoid cyclists. Ignore the paths to the right and left. Veer left towards the modern red brick King's Orchard House.

This area produced food for the royal court when it visited. A ferry was established near here in 1651 and was rented to the chamber, the predecessor of the council for 40 shillings per year. By the mid-18th century this had risen to £90 pounds as traffic increased. Whilst this author was researching another book, I was repeatedly struck by the apparent disinterest in finding a remedy to the congested and sometimes fatal roadway on the bridge. It seems the council was more interested in acquiring funds for their expensive dinners which were lost when the new bridge opened.

Pause on the small bridge and look to your left.

This was the site of the watergate as shown on the town seal from 1359. Sailing ships lowered their masts to fit under the old 4-arched Bristol Bridge. They passed here to unload supplies at a quay inside the castle. Beyond the castle to the east, the parish of St Phillip and Jacob, known as Pip'n'Jay, became an increasingly industrial suburb, with large distilleries, glass works and iron foundries. Much of their output was exported.

Retrace your steps up the slope. Turn right before you reach the cycle path again, to a stone structure with what looks like noses stuck to it.

These were drains in the castle's 2 metre thick stone wall. They are interspersed with arrow slits to repel water-borne invaders. A chute low down on the wall was the outlet for the garderobe, or toilet. It is impossible to see the site of the original water line. It was a sloping mud bank, long absorbed into eighteenth and nineteenth century quay walls.

Continue along this path, up the steps made of old railway sleepers. Turn right onto the cycle path. At the way markers by the bandstand, turn left then immediately right. Head towards a small brick building.

Though unassuming and modern-looking, these two rooms were probably porticoes to the King's Hall. It bustled with activity when the monarch and his large retinue visited Bristol. Columns in the room on the right are in the 13th century 'stiff leaf' style, like those in St Mary Redcliffe and the cathedral. These are not made of stone, but are terracotta discs mortared together.

The open space to your left was the main castle precinct. After the Civil War, Cromwell ordered the castle 'slighted'.

From the late 17th to early 18th centuries the open spaces filled up with gardens, then houses and businesses. They were mostly owned by members of various Nonconformist religious groups. Churchman's factory produced patented chocolate at Castle Mill before 1731. The company later became Fry's. Champion's porcelain works, one of the first in the country, was sited here between 1768 and 1782. Examples of its wares survive in the museum on Park Street. Imperial Tobacco began here as Wills in 1786. By the mid-18th century, most of the wealthy merchants, such as the Goldneys had decamped to the healthier areas on the heights of Clifton and Kingsdown, leaving the old centre to continue its decay.

Follow the path round towards the shopping precinct. Veer right towards the castle wall.

On the right is a stone enclosure with strange ceramic fish on tiles, a survivor of the 1992 park. 'Only the Dead Fish Go with the Flow' by Victor Moreton and Ceramica do Dauro commemorates Bristol's once-flourishing trade with Portugal. Though cider is strongly associated with Somerset, port was the drink of choice in Bristol and was a major import. Poet Laureate John Betjeman recalled the pre-war inner city being full of bars selling port, reminding him of the Spanish Main. This is also near the site of Champion's works.

Facing the sculpture is a circular space in the wall, a lookout point.

In the thirteenth century the wall was two metres higher. Below it was a floodplain which became the suburb of Broad Mead by the River Frome in 1147.

Meads were low-lying water meadows which were flooded in spring to provide early grazing for animals, and harvests of hay. The

Dominicans or Black Friars built their church there in 1227–8 with gardens, beehives and orchards. Part of it became a merchant's house and was then adapted for various industries. The Cutlers' Hall of 1499–1770 was probably their dormitory. The Quakers used it for their school, hence the confusing name for the area of Quakers' Friars. The part that became Bakers' Hall also survives.

Turn left along the wall. The main path veers right to The Galleries. Continue straight ahead to an open area where you can read about the castle ruins on the information boards.

The original design of the Saxon castle was 'motte and bailey', i.e., a moat and outer wall. It was demolished about 1120 and replaced with the massive Norman stone keep, called 'the flower of all keeps in England'. Within the castle was a garrison, stabling, and a chapel dedicated to St Martin, patron saint of soldiers. The east side of the keep provided lodgings. It had "all that was needed to make life more comfortable and to enable the occupants to withstand long sieges". It was still a big draughty stone box, but a safe one, with large fires and heavy tapestries to try to keep out the cold.

To the right, about where the Gothic style former conveniences now stand, was the Newgate Prison.

A plaque on the Union Street entrance to The Galleries commemorates the death of the self-proclaimed genius poet Richard Savage. He was imprisoned for a small debt after locals tired of his freeloading. His poem to Bristol includes the lines:

> "Thy sons! tho' crafty, deaf to Widsom's call,
> Despising all men, and despis'd by all;
> Sons! while thy cliffs a ditch-like river laves,
> Rude as they rocks, and muddy as thy waves,
> Of thoughts as narrow as of words immense,
> As full of turbulence and void of sense?"

The mason and architect Francis Greenaway was sentenced to death for fraud. But he had forged a signature to save a colleague from bankruptcy, so was reprieved and transported to Sydney where he became the father of Australian architecture. He was commemorated on the country's $10 note. In 1787 the Society for the Relief of Insolvent Debtors funded the release of F.C.M.G Maratt Amiatt, an itinerant teacher and quack who had run up debts. He was not heard of again, but was later identified as Jean Paul Marat, murdered in his bath in 1793 by Charlotte Corday.

You are now within sight of the start of the walk.

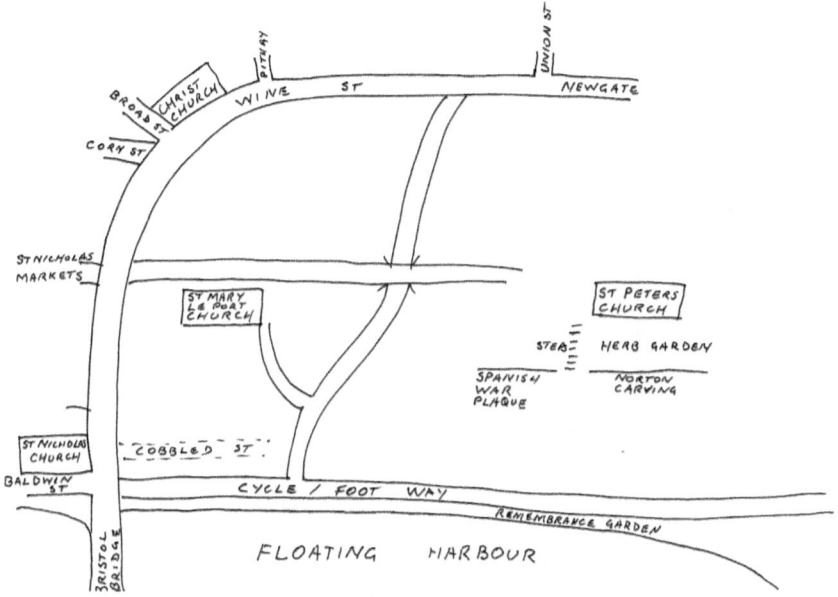

TWO

Norman Town

Start: Entrance to Castle Park, opposite The Galleries shopping centre

End: The walk is circular
Length: Approx 1km/ 0.75 mile
Route: Entirely in public park. Several gentle slopes, one flights of steps at end which can be diverted around
Public Transport: Any buses to city centre/Broadmead/Old Market

PREAMBLE

The king owned the castle and spent much money maintaining it and the garrison, but he was often absent. Disputes arose between his constable and the locals. In 1312 the townspeople besieged the castle in the 'Burgess' Revolt'. By 1373 the town and its merchants were the major power in the region, and were granted a charter in recognition of this.

The Domesday Book records a church here, but it is unclear which it was, either at the crossroads or here, St Mary-le-Port or St Peter's. The latter saint is depicted holding the keys to heaven, and that church was closest to the castle. Taxes and government business were enacted there and it served as an intermediary between the Crown and the town. The present church was built in the fourteenth century Perpendicular Gothic style. Many of the town's wealthiest merchants, often involved in the wool trade, were buried there, in tombs made of alabaster and jade. Behind the altar was a reredos carved by John Mitchell of London who worked on several of Wren's churches. By 1746 the Reverend Mr Hugh Waterman had been rector there for an impressive 57 years.

Most churches had their own water supply, the 'parish pump', where women gathered to exchange news and gossip as they waited their turn. In front of St Peter's was the ornate Gothic St Edith's Well which was famous for its fine water. It was funded by William Spencer, who as well as being mayor, was the executor of the 'merchant prince' and several times mayor William Canynge. After the Reformation, when most holy sites were vandalised or destroyed, the well was rebuilt in 1634 as St Peter's Pump. It was again housed in an ornate Gothic structure. But in 1775 it had become an obstruction to traffic so was moved by Henry Hoare to join the city's High Cross at his huge estate of Stourhead. Hoare's ancestors had lived in St Peter's parish, and at least one had been a mason so may have built or repaired the pump.

After the castle was demolished, its precincts were absorbed into the parish but they remained a separate, and increasingly lawless, electoral ward.

In past times, the River Avon was lined with the large houses of wealthy merchants. Ships unloaded goods directly to the houses' large cellars for storage. Some of the richest traders lived in Worshipful Street between the medieval stone bridge and the castle. The most famous house belonged to the Norton family and lay between the river and the graveyard of St Peter's church. Thomas Norton lived there in the early 15th century. He became one of only 3 lay alchemists in England. He "professed that art which ought not to be called an art, but rather the off-scourings of an idle mind". Alchemists are often seen as magicians or frauds, but kings often turned to them in the hope that they could produce much-needed gold. Norton's book, 'Ordinall of Alchemy' is in the British Museum. He claimed to have discovered both the philosophers' stone and the elixir of life. And yet he died. Two mansions which abutted the churchyard were owned by his relatives, 2 Aldworth brothers. One house was situated to the east, the other stretched to the water. Robert Aldworth was one of the city's richest and most important merchants. He replaced one of the buildings in 1612 as the grand mansion with fine carvings which was remembered by locals as St Peter's Poor House. It was destroyed in the Blitz.

War with France in the 17th century caused rising unemployment amongst local weavers. Merchant John Carey proposed the establishment of centralised poor houses. They were to employ the able-bodied poor, train the young, and care for the elderly and infirm. The poorhouse building was bought from Edward Colston and others.

Parts of it had been used as a sugar refinery and a mint. It became a model for the rest of the country. Its resident physician was Dr Dover, who had sailed with Woodes Rogers and invented Dr Dover's biscuits.

The scheme assumed the able-bodied poor would be able to support themselves. But residents were increasingly the old, the terminally ill, and the disabled, so the scheme cost more than expected. Parts of the building were old and unsanitary, so when cholera arrived in 1832, it killed many of its inhabitants. It was taken over by the corporation in 1920.

St Mary-le-Port was probably founded by William, Earl of Gloucester in 1170 t help fund the canons at Keynsham Abbey. It was a small parish, with only 76 houses to provide rents for its upkeep. In 1814, workmen repairing the church found an ancient lead coffin. The body inside was wrongly assumed to be the royal martyr, Robert Yeamans. The well-preserved body was dissected by surgeon and body snatcher Richard Smith. He collected information on executed criminals, which he recorded in books bound in their tanned skin.

William Hume was a Scottish snuff maker who lived in Mary-le-Port Street. In 1754 he bought Cotham windmill for grinding snuff, but three years later he advertised a bankruptcy sale of eleven mills. His business used a parrot sign. It became Ricketts, predecessors of the huge Wills tobacco company.

Both churches were badly damaged during World War II. Molten lead from the burning St Peter's church roof was said to have formed rivers running towards the water, hindering the work of firefighters. Both buildings were condemned for post-war demolition after their parishioners moved to new housing estates in the suburbs. But they were saved as part of Sir Kenneth Clark's plans to create landscaped gardens as memorials. It was hoped the churches would be included in the 1990s park as art spaces, but the funding was insufficient. In recent years locals have erected several war memorials on St Peter's front wall. Many locals who opposed the later plans for the park's redevelopment believed it was already a memorial site.

After Bristol Bridge was rebuilt in the 1760s, Bridge Street was laid out to improve access to the new bridge and with a plan for new properties to help pay off the costs of its construction. But by then the wealthy were moving to the fresh air and views of Kingsdown and Clifton. Those who remained were too poor to invest. Eventually the street was lined with four-storeyed Georgian houses rising up the gentle slope. They had warehouses and shops on the ground floor and cellars below. It was the first complete stone terrace built in the old city, and became the finest shopping street, but development was slow.

Near St Mary-le-Port church was the Bridge Street Presbyterian Chapel. It had an uphill entrance and cellars rented out to merchants dealing in alcohol. A poem noted that it had "spirit above and spirits below". The family of Elizabeth Blackwell worshipped there. and she heard stories of missionaries which inspired her to devote her life to good works. When her family left Bristol after the riots, despairing of the city's recovery, she became the first female doctor in the United States.

The bridge itself is a fascinating hybrid, with James Bridges' 18th century construction largely hidden by later additions. It is intact apart from the Portland stone balustrade. This was removed when the roadway was widened and its stone pillars partly obscured in the 1860s. The present steel parapet dates from the 1960s, so it seems every time Bristol's economy expands, the city widens its namesake bridge.

THE AMBLE

Start at the main entrance to St Peter's church with the memorials to the civilian dead of World War II. Skirt round to the right to the herb garden.

A range of medieval medicinal and culinary herbs grow here. Most of are Mediterranean, as the earliest monks came from France. Some locals believe the garden was to commemorate a medieval St Peter's Hospital which never existed. Other sources claim it was a leper hospital, but this is yet another urban legend. As with plague hospitals, such institutions were built outside urban centres. The garden is part of the park designed in the 1990s. It is now maintained by volunteers

CHAPTER TWO 17

On the wall of the church is a memorial to the self-proclaimed genius poet Richard Savage.

He died a pauper in nearby Newgate Prison and was buried in August 1743 in an unmarked grave somewhere in the churchyard. For some years it became a site of pilgrimage for his fans.

Between the garden and the river was the Tudor mansion of the Norton family.

A descendant, Robert Aldworth, bought it in 1607. He rebuilt much of it, complete with fine carvings of Jonah leaving the whale and Daniel in the lion's den. It was later owned by Aldworth's former apprentice William, father of Bristol's infamous benefactor Edward Colston. In 1696 it became the only sugar house in the city. In 1697 when this country was running out of coins, it was the major royal mint. Traders at the annual fairs exchanged their worn-out coinage for shiny new currency. Other mints were at Exeter, Chester and Norwich. It later became St Peter's Hospital, the country's first centralised poorhouse. Its wonderful carved wooden facade was one of the most tragic losses in The Blitz.

Return to the main entrance of St Peter's. Turn your back to it and head towards the ruins of the 15th century St Mary-le-Port church. The cellars of its priests' house have been exposed by wartime bombing.

The street may have been a Saxon hollow or holy way, part of the main route through the town and possibly a bypass when Wine Street markets were held. Archaeologists have found late Saxon and early Norman pottery nearby and traces of iron smelting and leather working.

St Mary-le-port was a small parish church that was entered through an ornate archway on the narrow St Mary-le-Port Street. Records from 1750 claim a mooring post was removed from inside the north door of the church, i.e., the one furthest from the water. Rents on houses built against the church wall provided the parish's main income. A painting by the artist John Piper, on display at Tate Britain shows this church after it was bombed. Sir Kenneth Clarke, head of the War Artists Advisory Committee, commissioned it as part of a series to boost morale. It was also used on a Royal Mail stamp.

Piper's painting of Coventry Cathedral has been called 'Britain's Guernica'.

Head down the slope to the water's edge to see Bristol Bridge, the city's namesake.

Before the quay wall was built, the medieval Worshipful Street ran along the muddy waters' edge. Ruinous Gothic buildings became the Butcher's Shambles, with cellars extending almost under St Mary's churchyard. They were partly swept away by floods in 1739, and later demolished when Bridge Street was laid out. The butchers were forced to move to St Nicholas' Market when it was built behind the Exchange on Corn Street.

Walk along the nearest of two riverside paths, the former Bridge Street.

The lower cobbled street was Back Bridge Street. It became popular for promenading and fresh air in the crowded 19th century inner city. This is now a pedestrian path and cycle route. A large fig tree grew over the water from the quay wall, a successful exotic import.

Further along, on the right, is a garden of remembrance for the D-Day landings.

It was sponsored by the Courage Brewery, which was across the water, the last major industrial site in the city centre. It took over Georges' Brewery which began there in the late 18th century. It closed in 2000 to become yet another expensive housing development.

Turn left towards the steps leading up to St Peter's.

To the left on the abutment is a memorial to local members of the International Brigade who died in the Spanish Civil War. The conflict gave German troops experience so they were battle-ready at the outbreak of World War II.

The plaque is surrounded by a ceramic in the International Brigade colours. It was erected by the local trades unions, and for many years a nephew of one of the fallen worked as Castle Park's gardener. Beside it is a smaller plaque erected by the Bristol Trades Union Council and Bristol Labour Party to workers who lost their lives as volunteers in the war. As Britain was not then involved in the conflict, those who returned were treated as criminals.

To the right of the path is a carving of the head of Thomas Norton, builder of the original Great House, though no image survives of him. It was funded by a local arts group hoping to encourage public access in the 1970s when the area was still a wasteland.

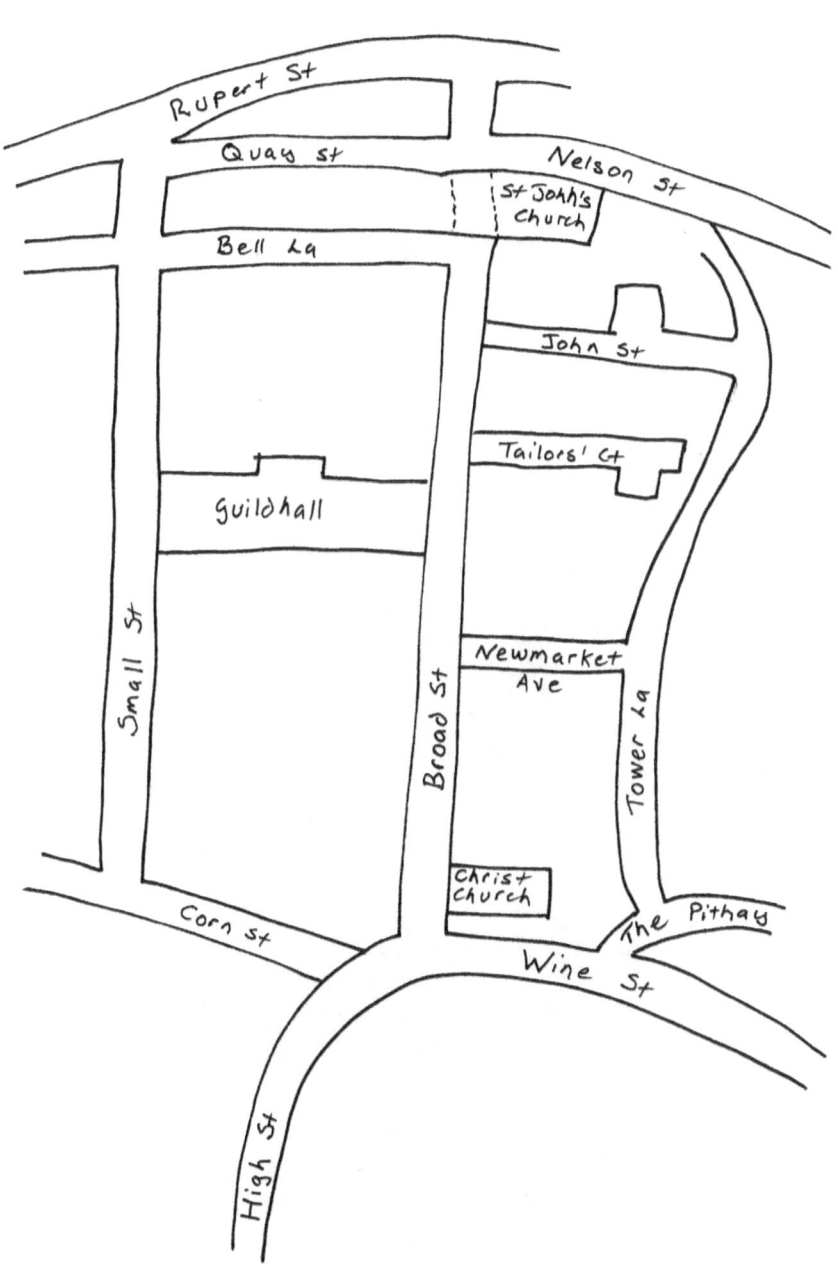

THREE

Merchant's Town
    Start: Corner of Corn Street and Broad Street
    End: Corner Corn Street and Small Street
    Length: Approx. 0.5km/0.25 mile

Route: Quiet back streets and lanes. A few gentle slopes but no steps

Public Transport: Any buses to city centre

PREAMBLE

Bristol's medieval town centre was at the crossroads where High, Wine, Broad, and Corn Streets meet. The churches of St Ewen's, Christ Church and All Saints occupied 3 of its corners. The famous ornately carved, five-storey Tudor timber townhouse of 1676 was called the Dutch House which was damaged in the Blitz. Claims were made that it could have been preserved, but this was not a priority when so many people were homeless.

The town's brightly painted and gilded high cross stood in the centre of the intersection. It celebrated the granting of Bristol's charter in 1347 which gave the citizens various rights to trade as an independent town. Whenever a new monarch was crowned, the town authorities asked for the charter to be reconfirmed. The cross displayed statues of the monarchs who confirmed and extended these important rights. It was a major landmark, and a site of public proclamations, celebrations and punishments. Markets were held at the base of the cross and spread into surrounding streets. High Street was known as Cooks' Row due to the many fast food outlets which catered for market traders and customers.

The cross was taken down in 1733 for being an obstruction to traffic and stored in the Guildhall. In 1735 it was re-erected in the centre of College Green where it was repaired and "finely beautified". But in 1763 the area was called the Mall of Bristol, so it was taken down as an obstruction to promenading pedestrians. Its pieces were stored in the Cathedral from where the banker Henry Hoare transported it to his estate at Stourhead, now a National Trust property. The much eroded figures survive, still showing traces of their colours, on the main staircase in London's V&A Museum.

Wine Street was only 11 feet wide at the main intersection, but it broadened out to become spindle shaped to make space for its market. It was the main north-south route through the town. The first guard house was here, and was replaced with the first police station. The street briefly had a market house and water pump in its centre. By the late 18th century, the market house had been long deserted so the council rented it out as a cheese market and for a short time the upper room was a school. With so much passing traffic, the street had some of the finest shops in the area, especially for drapers. The father of Edward Colston lived there for many decades. Poet Laureate Robert Southey was born there and baptised in Christ Church.

Broad and Small Streets were home to many wealthy merchants' houses. Diarists John Evelyn and Samuel Pepys called them "palaces". Street frontages were prime real estate. Sites were narrow and extended backwards with gardens, workshops, stables, kitchens and dungheaps. The sole surviving example of such a house is on this walk.

THE AMBLE
Begin at the corner of Broad Street and pedestrianised Corn Street.
Thomas Paty repaired the decaying medieval Christ Church in the late 1780s. The present structure, of 1792, is by his eldest son William, the first local graduate of the Royal Academy. It is modelled on London's St Martin in the Fields, but its interior was painted navy and grey. It is smaller than its predecessor as the council demanded Wine Street should be widened and Broad Street improved. Quarter jacks on the clock ring out the quarter hours. They are from the previous church and were by James Paty, probably father to Thomas. The high windows faced Wine Street so shops could be built against the church wall. Their rents provided income for the parish. The design also helped keep out the street noise during church services. This was also the main reason for its large porch. The parish is now combined with St Ewen, All Saints, and St George, and the church continues to hold services based on the 1662 Prayer Book.

On the opposite corner of Broad Street is the Grade II listed Old Council House of 1823 by Robert Smirke. It replaced a smaller building dating from 1701. The tiny church of St Ewen with its hedged churchyard was also demolished. The Council House was extended in 1898, replacing three houses on Broad Street. This provided a new chamber and magistrates' court. On the Corn Street pediment is a figure of Justice by prolific Bristol-born artist E.H. Bailey, or Baily, who was responsible for the statue of Nelson in Trafalgar Square. Justice held a sword but no scales which was said to be an astute observation about the council. But weather damage has removed even this; she now holds only a shield. Several of Baily's pieces are in the city's art gallery and on the pediment of the Freemasons' Hall. He was silversmith to Queen Victoria, but of course he is unknown in his native city.

The building became redundant when the new Council House was built on College Green. The 43 years of planning this took was incredible even by Bristol standards. The Old Council House is now a venue for hire.

Proceed down Broad Street.

On the right is the Thistle Hotel. It was built as the Grand Hotel in 1864 by Foster and Wood who took over the Paty business. It replaced the White Hart Inn, one of the great coaching inns. It provided lodgings for the Somerset family, the Dukes of Beaufort, when they visited the city, and was a base for their High Church Tory supporters during elections. In the hotel corridor are framed historic documents and the basement bar has a medieval well. Running alongside it is Newmarket Avenue, where servants from local houses shopped for food. It was the site of a lock-up destroyed in the 1831 riots.

On the left of Broad Street is the former branch of the Bank of England, designed by Charles Cockerell from 1846. On the right at no. 51 is a fine Byzantine-style building, originally the Avon Fire Office of 1868. By Pontin & Gough, it is a precursor to their famous Granary on Welsh Back.

The large building on the left is the Guildhall, of 1843 by R.S. Pope which replaced the too-small medieval hall where Judge Jeffries had held his Commission into the Monmouth Rebellion, better known as 'the Bloody Assizes'. But the uprising was stopped before it reached Bristol, and he only condemned 6 men for high treason, of whom 3 were reprieved. Pevsner described the present building as England's oldest Perpendicular town hall. When completed, it was condemned for being too small and poorly ventilated. It resembles the Houses of Parliament at Westminster.

On the right, go through the cobbled archway of a 15th century house, the former Guildhall Tavern, into Taylors' Court.

The rear of the building has jetties. They were necessary in some tall wooden buildings to act as counterbalances to prevent the floors from sagging. Many old buildings became wider as they were built upwards. This deprived the streets below of light, but made it easier to throw rubbish onto the roadway. This wall has two rare, defaced statues, possibly of angels. They may have been on the inside of a pre-Reformation domestic chapel.

Along the left side of the courtyard is the former Merchant Taylors' Hall, rebuilt in 1740. It had storage and workspace on the ground floor and a banquet hall above. Its fine shell hood shows the head of John the Baptist, patron of this and several other local guilds. Prancing camels represent their involvement in the Levant silk trade. They were a wealthy and powerful group. In 1701 the guild built an almshouse on Merchant Street with 9 rooms for elderly and infirm members; their wives and widows were given 3 shillings per week. The building is now part of The Galleries shopping centre. For many years they struggled to maintain their membership, so hired out the hall for public exhibitions and entertainments. The guild became extinct in 1824 on the death of the last member. For many years he had continued their traditions, electing himself master and paying himself to attend meetings and to keep the books. This seems to have been eccentric behaviour, but on his death, it was exposed as fraud. In the 1860s Bible Christians held their meetings here.

At the rear of the court on the right is the large Court House of 1692. The initials of its owner James Freeman are on the shell hood. An excavation at the end of the court revealed the remains of a Norman storehouse with stables, 15th century trade tokens from Venice and Germany, tin-glazed bowls from Spain and a bottle stopper made from a horse's tooth.

At the end of the court on the left is the graveyard of St John's church. Along with the city's other burial grounds, it was closed under the 1854 Health in Towns Act.It has an ornate tomb to the Brown family of the parish and an adjoining stone which has poetry suggesting the departed had suffered financial and other hardships.

Facing this is St John's churchyard, where a fine tomb is visible through the railings. It commemorates the Browne family and resembles a conduit house; it shelters the effigy of Edmund Browne and his wife. He was a local merchant who died in 1637 aged 83. Attached to it is a plaque dedicated to his son who was born in 1606. He became treasurer of the Merchant Venturers and was several times their master, and also mayor. He died in 1653. The plaque bears the following epitaph, suggesting he suffered terrible misfortune, probably from the Civil War:

"Things here are subject unto change
Merchants like to their ships do sayle
At first with prosperous wind yet faile
At last if God makes Storms to Rise
And shipwreck humane enterprise."

It has recently been restored and is open to the public again.
Retrace your steps and turn right into Broad Street. Pass a row of shops.
They seem to have 18th century brick facades but they may be much older.
Turn right into St John's Street.
This was laid out in the mid-18th century to improve the area and increase revenues for the parish. Today this would be called gentrification. The buildings on the right side are fine survivors of the period. Towards the end on the left is a lovely Victorian terracotta building.
Look up to see a dragon drinking from the top of a drainpipe.
Further along is the Bank pub, also one of the street's original buildings.

At the far end is Tower Lane which ran inside the old town wall. Beyond it was St John's almshouse, built by Robert Strange when mayor in the 15th century, funded by rents from Castle Mill on the river Frome near Newgate. It was rebuilt in 1721 for women who were funded by poor rates.

Retrace your steps and turn right into Broad Street.

On the right is the former printing works of Edward Everard, a rare local example of art nouveau, from 1901. Everard's name is displayed on the facade in his own typeface. The Spirit of Literature separates Gutenberg and Morris. Above them a woman holds a lamp and a mirror, representing light and truth. The design was by J R Neatby, and it is the largest decorated facade of its kind in England.

The street ends at the Grade I listed St John-on-the-Wall, or St John the Baptist. It is the city's only surviving gateway and has a portcullis slot. The tower has weathered statues possibly from the seventeenth century, of Brennus and Bellinus, the city's legendary Trojan or British founders. The arms of the Merchant Venturers and the Stuarts can also be seen. The tower was shared with the church of St Lawrence.

The River Frome was beyond the gate. But in the 13th century it was diverted and the old town walls became redundant for defence. Four churches, including St Nicholas, were built within them. St John's dates from c.1350–1500. It was funded by Walter Frampton, 3 times mayor whose tomb survives inside, showing his feet resting on a dog. This demonstrates the immense wealth of merchants at the time, mostly from the wool trade. The pedestrian passageways are Victorian. The original church and crypt entrance was within the main gateway.

Go through the archway and turn right to see the lion-headed conduit head which has been recently restored.

You will pass the vaulted crypt which is sometimes open to the public. It was dedicated to the Guild of the Holy Cross. A 13th century conduit ran from Brandon Hill to the Carmelite friary. It has a reservoir under the pavement halfway up Park Street which is marked by an incised stone. Its original outlet was in an ornate Gothic house inside the wall, the site of the present door. During the Blitz, the main water supply from Bedminster was bombed, so this became the only source of water for the area.

The church is managed by the Churches Conservation Trust, and is sometimes open to the public for music and art displays. Check their website for opening details. You can make a donation to this worthy charity, or even become a member.

When Edward I expelled the Jews from England in 1290, a few remained in Bristol. They lived outside the wall on the edge of the Frome between St John's and St Giles' gates. Their synagogue was in the abandoned crypt of the latter. Before that, in 1275, the area had become a gathering place for those driven from Gloucester.

Retrace your steps through the archway. Turn right along the cobblestoned Leonard's Lane, taking care with traffic.

This follows the inside of the old town wall. About half way along on the right are some lead markers. These are boundary markers for the parish of St John and the former parish of St Lawrence. Similar markers can be seen throughout the old city. They were guides for the annual perambulation of the parish to confirm its boundaries.

The lane continues through the archway of an old house. But before this, turn left into Small Street and proceed up the hill. Most of the right-hand side is the facade of the Old Post Office, which moved from Corn Street next to the Exchange. It was built in 2 stages as the postal system expanded. The section to the left of the central arch is by James Williams and dates from 1887–9, while that on the right is by E G Rivers who had to follow the same style. The final extension was added in 1908–9. The facade was kept when the building became the Crown Court in 1994.

About halfway up on the left is a plaque for Foster's Chambers. It was the home of 15th century merchant John Foster who served as mayor and founded the almshouse at the top of Christmas Steps. Bristol is full of nonsensical stories of underground tunnels, but beneath this building, there is a series of cellars. Many were rented out for storage, either singly or as groups, so they are joined together. They allegedly extend almost as far as the bridge.

At one of the first Doors Open Day events, the cellars were lit with flickering candles and echoed with organ music. The owner described how he used to amuse himself by opening trap doors into the offices above, terrifying legal secretaries. As you do.

Set back from the street adjoining this is the Assize Court, by Pope and Bindon of 1867–70. It was built to remedy the lack of space at the old Guildhall with which it connects. It resembles Brunel's Temple Meads station. It incorporated part of a 12th century hall house. Despite claims that it was owned by the Colston family, making it the last of the city's merchant palaces, this was demolished in 1961. At the time it was claimed by Pevsner: "even in Bristol there are few pieces of Corporation vandalism to match it".

On the right-hand corner of Small Street and Corn Street was the medieval church of St Werburgh's, a parish with only about 46 houses, but many were wealthy. It was named after a little-known abbess famous for her kindness to animals, especially geese. Her church in Chester became the cathedral there. As the parish was home to some of the city's richest merchants, the memorials in it were some of the finest. They include one of the city's 2 royal martyrs, George Boucher who was hanged by the Parliamentarians in 1643. Another was to one of the city's great benefactors, Nicholas Thorne, founder of Bristol Grammar School. His large stone was removed to decorate a gentleman's gothic stable. As James Bridges was employed on both this church and Arnos Court at Brislington, it probably ended up there. In the chancel was an inscription to the merchant Humphrey Brown, who died in 1630. His name suggests he was one of many welsh people who came to England in the wake of the Tudors to make their fortunes. He was perhaps a relative the family in St John's burial ground, and his wife Elizabeth White, with the inscription:

"Here lies a Brown a White, the colours one
Pale drawn by Death, here shaded by a stone:
One house did hold them both whilst life did last,
One grave do hold them both now live is past."

By 1757 the church was declared unsafe but the small parish could not afford to rebuild it, so a nationwide subscription was raised. But it was still an obstruction to traffic on both streets, especially when the post office expanded in the 19th century. It was removed in 1877 and partly rebuilt in the parish which bears its name beside the M32. It is now a Grade II* listed climbing centre.

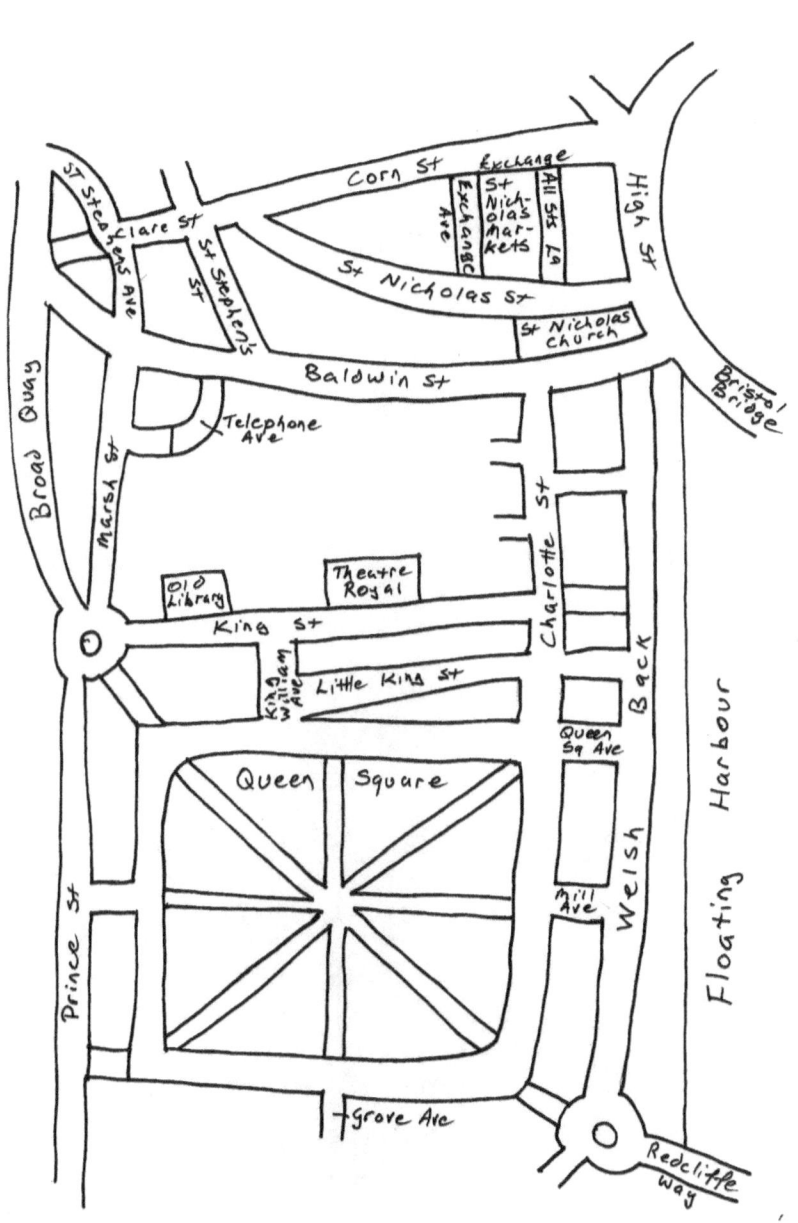

FOUR

Georgian City

Start: Corn Street, between Broad Street and Small Street
End: Queen Square
Length: Approx. .0.75km/0.5 mile
Route: A mixture of pedestrianised streets and mixed traffic areas. No slopes or steps Public Transport: Any buses to the centre

PREAMBLE

Much of early 18th century Bristol was still medieval, with no major building projects for over two centuries. It also suffered extensive damage by both sides in the Civil War. Streets were crowded, dirty, and dark from overhanging buildings. Many were only wide enough for packhorses, so they were unfit for the increasing number of coaches, sledges and farm wagons. The many street markets added to the congestion and to the filth.

But in the first decades of the century the city's fortunes began to improve. The new Council House was funded by profits from speculative building on King Street and the Castle Precincts. Queen Square was the first planned development. It was also the first to specify high quality materials and building standards, reducing the risks of fire. Uniformity of design echoed the pattern of nearby Bath. It enhanced the views across the central open space which encouraged social interaction. 'Noysome professions' were banned, as houses were for residential use only. This confirmed it as an elite address.

At the same time, the council used its powers as landlord to order buildings, especially on corners, to be cut back when tenancies were renewed. Thus as the city expanded, many buildings became smaller, which accelerated the exodus of wealth to the suburbs.

High Street was the main thoroughfare as it led downhill from the centre to the main bridge and quays. In the 18th century it was called 'Cooks Row' due to the many food outlets for market visitors and traders. From 1791 Joseph Cottle was a bookseller there. He became the friend and publisher of the poets Southey and Coleridge. The pair planned to settle in North America in an idealised society called the Pantisocrats. Robert Lovell was a Quaker and lesser-known member. He claimed the Susquehannah in North America only worked 2 hours per day, which would have left the poets plenty of leisure time to practice their art.

All Saints was one of the oldest churches in the city but very small and complex. A small house intruded into the fabric, supported by stone pillars. The tower was rebuilt in 1716, almost half the £589 was provided by Edward Colston as it was his father's parish. It previously housed the library of the Kalendary priests, under which was the parish conduit house and a house for the vicar. It housed several chantries or altars where prayers were said for the souls of their donors. At the Reformation, the church owned £4823 of silver plate. Josiah Tucker, famous author and abolitionist, was vicar here from 1739–49.

John Wood's Exchange on Corn Street, built in 1741–3, is described by Pevsner as his "most outstanding public building". He rated it highly as an example of 18th century architecture. Trade was carried out under the open colonnade of the Tolzey which was built against the wall of All Saints church. But for years complaints were made of it being overcrowded and exposed to street dirt and the elements. It was for merchants who dealt in wholesale trade, as opposed to shopkeepers.

In 1717 the city began its long discussion over a replacement, and William Halfpenny and George Tully submitted plans. The building was to be large, complex, and made of fashionable Bath stone, floated down the recently improved River Avon.

The 1740s was 'the lost decade of architecture' when an agricultural depression followed the collapse of the South Sea Bubble. This put a halt to the building of country houses. The council could have had their pick of the country's finest surveyors. Yet despite the importance of the project, the council showed their usual incompetence with long delays. They even asked Ralph Allen and his mason, before inviting John Wood of Bath at the last minute. He was often unreliable and, as a member of the hated Freemasons, was unpopular with the local workmen. Wood claimed local tradesmen were incompetent, but they built basic stone boxes, designed and supervised by a master builder. This was a large, complicated building, fronted with offices, and with ground-floor coffee and ale houses above a reservoir in case of fire. The huge size meant that half the masons employed were local, but they distrusted the Bath masons for being Freemasons like Wood.

Captain Foy was Clerk of Works and possibly a Methodist. He called the project "a piece of work, not workmanship". It was one of the first sightings of Thomas Paty, as an ornament carver. Behind The Exchange, they built one of the country's first arcade markets. It was based on that of Oxford and designed by local carpenter Samuel Glascodine. It had 3 covered halls: the East Arcade and the Gloucestershire and Somerset Markets. The huge arched entrance to the High Street had side entrances for pedestrians and housed stalls for flower sellers. It is aligned with Mary-le-Port Street. To the rear, facing St Nicholas Street, was the Butchers' Shambles. The tradesmen were forced to move here from the riverside of what is now Castle Park. A major inn was destroyed, and several pubs were altered and improved. The adjoining parish church of All Saints suffered huge inconvenience from dust and fears of collapse, and its conduit had to be moved.

The Exchange became a corn market in 1813. In 1869 E M Barry added an extra storey supported by carved caryatids but these are now obscured by the modern roof. Like the rest of the city centre, the market fell into disuse when trams were introduced to allow people to escape to the Victorian suburbs. The building became a skating rink and a rock venue until it was revived as a public market in recent decades. Nearby the first hackney cab stand was established in 1786. It began with three cabs but soon expanded to twenty.

In the 1770s Clare Street was laid out to connect the commercial centre of Corn Street with the main international quay, now The Centre. The street is named after Bristol's MP of 1754–74, Robert Craggs-Nugent, Lord Clare, who contributed to the development. He was an Irish politician and poet who served the city and St Mawes in Cornwall long enough to become the Father of the House. As Robert Nugent, he grew rich by marrying wealthy women who conveniently died, for which Horace Walpole coined the term 'nugentism'. A large portrait of him by Thomas Gainsborough is in Bath's Holburne

Museum. The street was funded by subscription which raised £8,000, of which the corporation provided £500, and £1,000 was lent by Lord Clare. When the street was completed in 1775 plot sales raised over £9,000. It required the demolition of many ruinous old buildings inhabited by the poor, so it was also a means to clear away slums, in an early form of gentrification. In the 19th century, banks and insurance offices replaced the old pubs and shops. They have, in turn, been replaced by pubs and student accommodation.

Corn Street led to St Leonard's church which was situated above a strange and increasingly dangerous 3-way gate in the town wall which led from Corn Street to Baldwin Street and the biggest gate to the quay. Part of its floor was timber but the rest was stone so the dead could be interred there. It was demolished in 1774 to build Clare Street, designed by Thomas Paty and constructed between 1771 and 1775. The new street was lined with fine houses above shops, some of which survive, such as no. 10, which have been joined by some equally fine, more modern buildings such as the terracotta Prudential Building of 1899.

King Street is named after Charles II. It was built as part of the city's recovery after the Civil War when the walls were no longer necessary for defence. It was the first street to be built outside the city walls and its uneven course shows it was not surveyed and formally laid out. Barratt claims there were 3 fairs for the sale of wool here each year, which seems odd; it may refer to Old King Street, now Merchant Street. King Street was home to many ships' captains and maritime trades which moved here as the port expanded downstream. Most of the buildings were speculatively, often built by shipwrights. Claims are often made that they include recycled pieces of ships and even barrel staves, but this is yet more Bristol nonsense. The street signalled the port's move downstream as ships involved in international trade, especially in the Atlantic, grew in size and in numbers. They moored on the new quay, now The Centre.

King Street is the site of the city's best collection of merchants' houses, with interesting later warehouses. After World War II, it was promoted as 'Museum Street' on Great Western Railway posters.

On the corner of Merchant Street is Merchant House. A plaque states that a guild of merchant mariners founded in 1445 maintained a priest and 12 poor seamen. Their Chapel of St Clement stood on this site. In 1553 the disused (i.e., dissolved by Henry VIII) chapel became the Hall of the Society of Merchant Venturers. This is a rare example of a religious foundation surviving the Reformation to the present day. Their organisation was confirmed but not necessarily approved of by Queen Elizabeth I. The hall was rebuilt on the same site in 1719 in an L shape with large well-lit rooms above working spaces. In 1940 it was destroyed by enemy action. Figures from the old hall can be seen on a shop halfway up Christmas Steps.

The Venturers are condemned for allegedly being a secret society which controls local government. They were infamous for their prolonged campaigning and support for the Atlantic slave trade. They are also accused of obstructing demands for the removal of Edward Colston's statue on The Centre.

Their hall was a working building where they held meetings and conducted business. It was also hired out for special dinners. They promoted the training and education of members' sons for maritime trades. They supported members in distress and maintained the adjoining almshouse for the elderly and infirm, including widows. They became responsible for the maintenance of the port and their members were exempt from paying port dues. Their detailed records on shipping were accessed by Thomas Clarkson and provided evidence of the high fatality rates of crews on slave ships, which helped the campaign for abolition.

King Street was home to one of the first public libraries in the country, when Robert Redwood donated a building to the city in 1614. Tobias Matthew donated his collection of mostly ecclesiastical books in his will when he died in 1628 for the benefit of aldermen and shopkeepers. He was born on Bristol Bridge and became Bishop of Durham and Archbishop of York. But by the mid-18th century, the library was seldom visited by anyone. Much of the collection came from the legacies of local clerics, meaning it was mostly religious tracts. Its museum collections included some rocks which allegedly proved the truth of Noah's flood.

Benjamin Donn who later added an e to his name, was the first person to win an award for drawing an accurate map of a county, his home of Devon. He became the librarian in 1765, but was so underemployed that he also ran a mathematical school there. In 1766 he produced an accurate map of Bristol, which he engraved and sold for extra income. He published books on accounting, navigation and mathematics and provided public lectures. Towards the end of his life he was appointed master of mathematics to the king. His geometrical models were praised by Dr Thomas Beddoes.

The subscription-funded Bristol Library Society was formed in 1772 to encourage use of the library. Bishop Newton was elected president. Donne was replaced by Reverend Thomas Johnes, vicar of St Johns, in 1773. The building was renovated by the corporation. Subscriptions allowed large purchases of popular books including many reference works. But the original collection was neglected and hard to access, so the public was effectively excluded.In 1786 the extra wing was added, again by Thomas Paty.

It was extremely popular and there was a constant struggle to find space for the new books. New shelving was built by the near-omnipresent Thomas Paty. Members included Southey, Coleridge, Wordsworth, Cottle, Dr Beddoes, Humphrey Davey, the engineer and educator R L Edgeworth and his daughter the novelist Maria. This shows how civilised and enlightened at least part of the city had become by the late 18th century. Robert Southey, who was born in Wine Street and often returned to his home town, claimed "I know of no mercantile place so literary".

The Town Marsh, or Waste, was south of the town walls, between the Frome and Avon rivers. It was originally farmland to support the Augustinian Abbey, which also owned properties in Bedminster and Trin Mills across the harbour. There had been long disputes over its ownership following the rerouting of the River Frome in the 14th centuries.

It had a wide range of uses before it was laid out as Queen Square, starting in 1699. Maps show sheep and cattle were fattened up for market there, and volunteers drilled in the use of arms. Near the water's edge ships were built and repaired in the mud docks. When Queen Elizabeth and later royals visited, a grandstand was built for them to see mock sea battles. In 1657 a bowling green was established, and trees planted for fresh air and promenading. When the square was laid out in 1699, it was the first example of urban planning by the corporation. It was one of the biggest squares in England.

The square was also home to the city's first mansion house, to accommodate the mayor. It was built in 1784 with a banqueting house behind on Charlotte Street.

The New Custom House was built there in 1709 and cost £2,777 7s 5d. During the Jacobite Rebellion of 1745 two London privateers landed prizes seized from two Spanish ships in July. The treasure was held in the Custom House and amounted to £1,476 hundredweight of gold which was valued at an incredible £727,372 17s. With other seized goods, it was transported to London in 22 wagons under heavy armed guard. But the building was burnt in the riots and all its records lost. Its replacement survives.

The famous 1831 riots began there. These were the largest and the last civil disturbance of 19th century Britain. The mayor was the young and inexperienced Liberal, Charles Pinney. The main protest was against the city recorder, Sir Charles Weatherall. Like the local bishop, he was against political reform. There are many accounts of the event, but the following suggests how strong the feelings of the rioters were. After Bishop Grey preached against the Reform Bill, he was chased by the mob to Knole Park at Over, in Gloucestershire. He allegedly retreated to "a long dark room some steps from the buttery called the Bishop's Cellar". He "hid from the mob shouting for his blood, whilst the servants stood by with muskets brought back from the Peninsular wars".

Over is about 6 miles (10 kilometres) as the crow flies from central Bristol. That's a very long way to stay angry.

THE AMBLE
Begin at John Wood's Exchange on Corn Street.

Along Exchange Alley to the right, and All Saints Alley to the left are former artisans' workshops with accommodation above. They were apparently the first of their kind in such a building. The inner court of the main building was open to the elements, following the design of exchanges in London and Antwerp.

The Exchange's interior with its craft stalls and the food stalls of the Glass Market behind are worth exploring.

Look up to see brightly painted carvings or plasterwork of the 3 corners of the earth.

The merchants' insistence on not putting a roof on the building confirmed architect John Wood's belief in their ignorance. Bath had shown how the provision of clean, wide streets lined with grand houses improved public behaviour. The Exchange thus provided an improved space for commerce, but was also an attempt to improve public behaviour in a wider sense. Lack of supervision by Wood meant the various trades working on the building were not coordinated. The structure was repeatedly altered and rebuilt to correct mistakes.

In front of the Exchange are 4 brass pillars, or 'nails' dating from the 16th and 17th centuries. They had fronted the Merchants' Tolzey or exchange against the wall of All Saints church. Merchants sealed agreements and made payments here, hence the term 'pay on the nail'. They were moved from outside the Council House to their present site in 1771.

On 22 March 1813 Henry 'Orator' Hunt — later of Peterloo fame — gave a "demagogical performance" on 1 of the pillars. The following night a group of men pulled down the statue of the king by Nollekens in Portland Square and so damaged the work that it was not replaced. One of the protesters was sentenced to twelve months in prison.

Despite the huge expense of its construction, the Exchange was never popular with merchants. They continued to meet in the open until the Commercial Rooms were opened opposite in 1809.

To the right of the Exchange on the corner of Exchange Alley is the Old Post Office, of 1748. It was built by 2 carpenters: Samuel

Glascodine and Daniel Millard junior. It began as a single house, possibly designed by post master Pyne, who rented it for £40 per year. As the postal business grew, the building extended down the alley to include horse stabling. When the site became too small, the post office moved to Small Street in 1865. On the other flank of the Exchange is a matching building by Thomas Paty of 1782. It was built into the fabric of All Saints church and replaced an earlier coffee house where the priest's house had been. For many years it was the stamp office run by various Samuel Worralls. One of them gained fame for taking in, and being taken in by, the fraudster Princess Caraboo in 1817.

Immediately opposite the Exchange is the glorious Bath stone Lloyds TSB bank by Lysaght & Gingell, of 1854–7. The bank's design was based on St Mark's Library in Venice, and the carvings represented the towns it served. A plaque records that it replaced the Bush Inn, run by the larger-than-life 18th century patron John Weeks. It was famous for his gargantuan dinners and potted turtles which when still alive were stored at his country house at Filton. The house became part of Bristol Aerospace, named after Admiral Rodney whose arrival in the city after the Battle of the Saints was celebrated there after a torchlit procession. Weeks was active in politics, raising funds for good causes, and he performed in charity shows at the Theatre Royal. He was one of the first to play the role of Mungo in the play 'The Padlock' by Charles Dibdin. Clarkson praised the play for its huge part in promoting abolition of the slave trade.

Walk towards The Centre and turn left into St Nicholas Street.

Several doors along on the left is a grand building in the old-fashioned Greek-temple style. On the pediment is the city's coat of arms with unicorns.

This was the 1903 Stock Exchange which was paid for by Sir George White, founder of the local aircraft industry. The ornate doorcase of 1637 is from St Mary the Virgin, Oxford. The interior has a spectacular art nouveau staircase which descends to impressive marble and mahogany sanitary facilities.

Further along is the Elephant pub of 1867, with an impressive carved elephant head set high on its facade. Opposite this is the former fish market, which replaced William Paty's market hall. It dates from 1873, by Pope & Son, who continued the Path family business.

On the rear wall of St Nicholas Market is a painted cast iron drinking fountain with the head of Queen Victoria. It was made by the Wills Brothers of London from the Coalbrookdale pattern book. It was one of several funded by grocer Mr Budgett in the first wave of public fountain building in 1859. It aimed to provide clean water after outbreaks of typhoid. It is Grade II listed.

Retrace your steps to Corn Street, turn left and continue along Clare Street towards the former Tramways Centre, now The Centre.

This was the main quay for overseas shipping from the 18th century. But by the late 19th century it was polluted so was covered over to accommodate the rise in vehicular traffic.

Before The Centre, turn left to cross Baldwin Street at the traffic lights into Marsh Street. This led to the Marsh Gate in the city wall. It opened onto pasture called the Town Waste which became Queen Square. It was lined with large medieval merchants' houses, but by the early 19th century the wealthy had abandoned the area for the healthier suburbs. The buildings decayed and became crowded homes for the poor, and houses of ill repute subject to raids by constables and the press gang. Many of the Irish navvies who helped build the New Cut and the floating harbour lived here. It still has some interesting buildings, and a detour to the left into Telegraph Avenue is worthwhile. At the end of the street is the modern Venturers' House. It is on the site of the hall of the now-infamous Merchant Venturers which was destroyed in the Blitz.

The Venturers are the city's last surviving guild, and are now based in a large mansion on the Promenade in Clifton. They are often seen as a secret power in the city, and in the wake of the Colston statue protests are now largely blamed for the delays in its removal. The Merchant Venturers built the adjoining almshouse in 1696 to care for aged and infirm mariners, as the now faded poem on the building describes.

"Freed from all storms the tempest and the rage

Of billows, here we spend our age.
Our weather beaten vessels here repair
And from the Merchants' kind and generous care
Find harbour here; no more we put to sea
Until we launch into Eternity.
And lest our Widows, whom we leave behind
Should want relief, they too a shelter find.
Thus all our anxious cares and sorrows cease
Whilst our kind Guardians turn our toils to ease.
May they be with an endless Sabbath blest
Who have afforded unto us this rest."

It had fresh air and fine views of the quays and beyond. The nearest wing was funded by Edward Colston in his will but was also lost in the Blitz.

Nearby on Princes Street, beside Assembly Rooms Lane was a popular assembly room where Latimer claimed "the young danced jigs and minuets, whilst their elders relaxed in "whisk" and card games now forgotten." Such events were also held in the Coopers' Hall when it was on Corn Street, and at the Merchants' Hall.

Continue round to the left into King Street.

Beside the almshouse is the old Library. The main wing facing the street dates from 1738 and cost the corporation £1600. It is attributed to James Paty, but he was only the stone mason. It was built by Daniel Millard junior, mason to the corporation. He employed many of the workers involved in building the Exchange, often for short periods. It may have been a job-creation scheme during the depression following the economic collapse of the South Sea Bubble. The wainscotting was made by sawing down floor timbers from a large inn that had been demolished to make way for the Exchange. On the top floor, to maximise light, was the main reading room with its ornate chimney-piece with overmantel. They have been attributed to the great baroque carver Grinling Gibbons, but may be by Thomas Paty. The room has been reconstructed upstairs in the Central Library Reference section and can be viewed on request.

The facade had ornate carvings of putti and the city arms, but these were destroyed during the 'repairs' of the 1970s. The wing at right angles to the street was also built by Thomas Paty in the 1780s when the Bristol Library Society took over the site. It was subsidised by rents from the ground-floor office.

Further down on the left is the Grade I listed Theatre Royal. Built in 1764-6 by Thomas Paty, it is Britain's oldest working theatre. It opened with 'The Conscious Lovers' with 'The Miller of Mansfield'. It was for the benefit of the Infirmary, a successful way of appeasing the magistrates and attracting audiences. The design was based on Drury Lane Theatre. Its auditorium is semicircular rather than the usual elliptical shape. It still has a 'thunder run', a trough down which cannon balls were rolled for sound effects.

Its entrance was through an alleyway and a house front. This is often claimed to have been to try to hide it from the public. But this is nonsense as the well-dressed crowds and their coaches were visible, and some of the original subscribers were Quakers. Like Wesley's New Room in Broadmead, it saved money by having no expensive street frontage.

The theatre opened in 1772, and David Garrick claimed it was the most complete theatre in Europe. The interior was painted by local Michael Edkins. Pevsner called it "internally a delight to the eye and in addition a most valuable document of English theatrical history". It was funded by shares and was built so fast that complaints were made that Paty's other project, St Nicholas Church, was being delayed. But the main entrance was not provided until the 1972 conversion which involved gutting the adjoining Coopers' or Hoopers Hall of 1733-4 and was opened up as a foyer for the theatre.

Plays were condemned for distracting apprentices from their duties and encouraging bad habits such as drinking and gambling. The Licensing Act of 1737 was passed in response to the widespread mockery of Robert Walpole, the first prime minister, and was not repealed until 1968. The theatre was unable to stage plays until granted its royal licence and name in 1778. But because it was licensed by the crown, it was outside the power of local magistrates so was able to keep whatever hours they chose.

In the late 18th century the theatre was run by John Palmer as a joint venture with the Bath Theatre Royal. He used large coaches to ferry cast and scenery between the two cities. He was later rewarded by the king for inventing the system of post-horses and went on to found the Royal Mail. But regular schedules made coaches easier prey for highwaymen so he was forced to employ armed guards.

Following the riots of 1831 the area went into longterm decline. The theatre also had to compete with the more populist Princes' Theatre on Park Row. During World War II it was used by the precursors of the Arts Council to provide entertainments for the troops, but it closed in 1942. A public appeal saved the building.

The Coopers' original hall had been demolished to make way for the Exchange, and this replacement was built by Yorkshireman William Halfpenny. He was a builder, and publisher of design books, including the first on chinoiserie. The hall was, like most guild halls, a ground floor working space with grand rooms above, as the Italian villas made popular by Palladio. But the guild went into decline, and increasingly rented out the upper floor for performances. In 1772 one of the strangest performances was held there when an Eskimo chief and his wife played the leads in Macbeth.

At the end of this block on the left is St Nicholas' almshouse. Dating from 1652, it is the oldest building in the street. The entrance hall is two storeys high. It had a chapel above, and its fine plaster ceiling with symbols of the Four Evangelists survives. In the rear courtyard is a bastion from the old town wall. It had no legacies to support the residents who were maintained by the poor rates.

Across Queen Charlotte Street is The Old Duke pub, named after Ellington It is famous for its New Orleans trad jazz and more modern styles.

On the opposite side of King Street is the Llandoger Trow pub, named after the Welsh boats that supplied fresh food to the city and moored on Welsh Back. It is often claimed to be the former haunt of pirates by people who have no idea what pirates were.

It was built c.1664 as a single townhouse in a line of 5, with warehouse basements. Some fine woodwork and fireplaces survive, including a German nativity scene overmantel. The 2 buildings closest to the water were destroyed in the Blitz. Anywhere else, this would be a museum.

Across the street is a brick-faced building from the same period.

During the war it was home to the Arts Council who were instrumental in getting King Street named and promoted as 'Museum Street'. It featured on Great Western Railway posters to encourage tourism, which probably saved it from the usual council vandalism.

Turn left into Queen Charlotte Street and proceed to Queen Square.

On the left corner of Little King Street is the Old Granary by Pontin and Gough, of 1869. It is the best surviving example of Bristol Byzantine and perhaps the finest Victorian building in the city. It was designed to be dark and draughty to preserve the grain. After many years as a legendary rock venue, it is now a restaurant and apartments.

The construction of Queen Square began in the 1690s. It had long been a common site for dumping the city's refuse until it 'rose like the creation out of chaos, to such beauty out of a muddy marsh'. In 1663 when the royal family had visited the city, they were entertained by the mayor. When they departed for Bath 150 guns were discharged on the marsh 3 times.

A building on the left as you reach the square, with a shell hood, shows the standards of building at the time. Opposite it, on the corner facing the square, was the house converted at great public expense in the 1780s to be the first mayoral residence. The recorder sought shelter there, at the start of the 1831 riots, so it became an early target for rioters when the young I K Brunel served as a constable.

The riots lasted were largely due to the authorities failing to intervene when the unpopular Recorder Sir Charles Wetherall arrived in the city. He opposed reform and claimed locals were not interested in politics. They began as a political protest but when this died down, a second wave took over, made up of freed criminals and attracting people from the cheap lodging houses in Marsh Street and further afield as news of the event spread.

In the centre of the square is J M Rysbrack's statue of the asthmatic William III of Orange as a Roman emperor. It is claimed to be the country's finest equestrian statue. But, being Bristol, there were many drawn out debates over whose statue should be chosen. Queen Elizabeth was popular and the most obvious was Queen Anne, or one of the many kings who had granted or extended the city's trading rights. William III was not a popular choice, and raising funds was slow and difficult. He may have been chosen as he abolished the Royal Africa Company's monopoly which opened up the Africa trade to ports such as Bristol. It was erected in 1736 after years of public fundraising but was paid off by the Merchant Venturers and the corporation.

At its base are worn parish boundary markers for St Nicholas' and St Stephens'. During the war, sheep grazed on the grass, and in the 1970s and '80s a road ran through the centre of the square, and traffic —including double decker buses — making windows in surrounding buildings rattle. The former Customs House on the middle of the north side was rebuilt after the 1831 riots when all its records were lost.

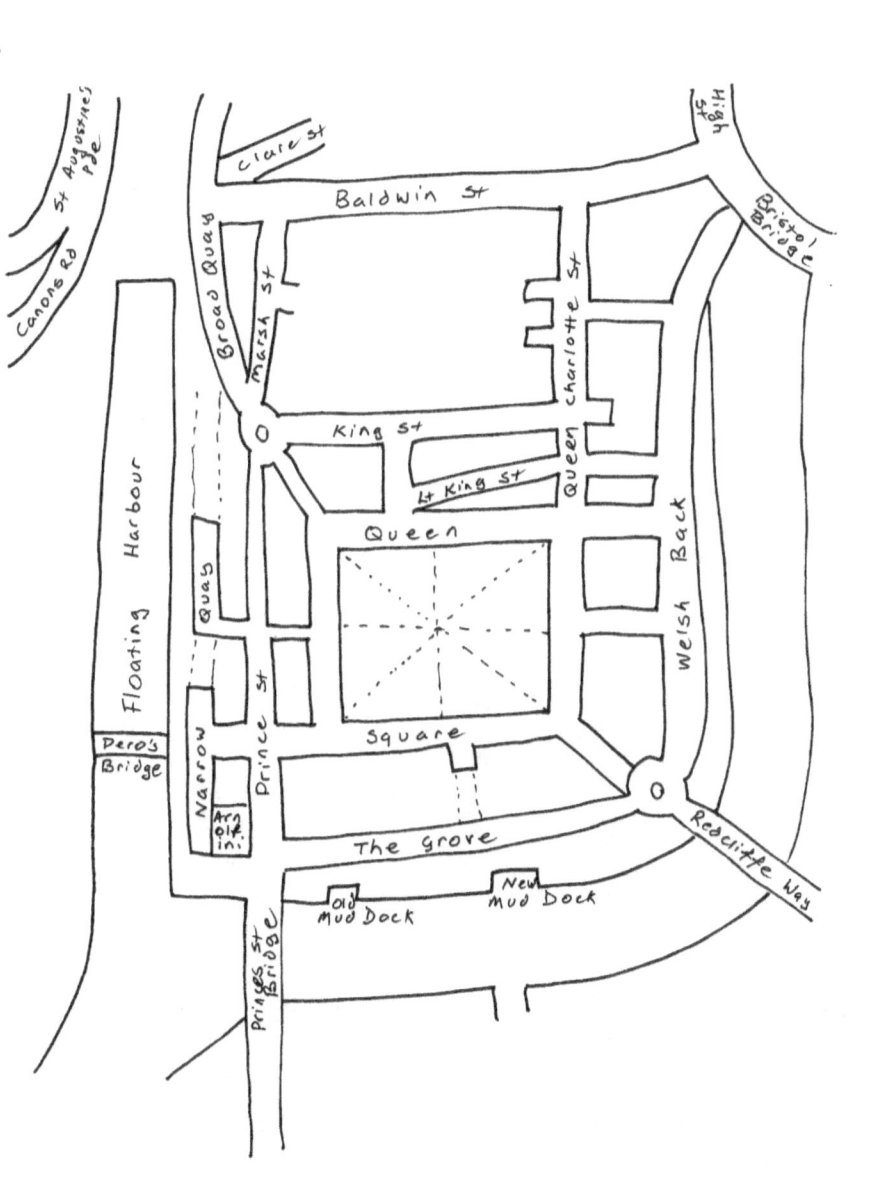

FIVE

Follow the Tide

Start: Corner of Welsh Back and Baldwin St beside Bristol Bridge
End: Centre/Colston Parade
Length: Approx. 1.5km/1 mile Route: A mixture of quiet back streets and pedestrianised areas. No slopes or steps.
Public Transport: Any buses to the city centre

THE AMBLE
Begin at the corner of Welsh Back and Baldwin Street.

The building here dates from the mid-19th century. It is by Thomas Paty, from a family who dominated the construction of Georgian Bristol. It retains some original features. Beside it is West India House, built by Oatley & Lawrence in 1902. It replaced the White Star Shipping Line's building. Somewhere here was the fourteenth century hall/home of the Spicer family. John Spicer was the town's first mayor in 1353. The Fellowship of Merchants had a chapel and meeting room there. Part of its ornate door survives in the city museum.

Along the water's edge are several floating restaurants. Four iron pillars are probably the remains of a covered market for oysters. It was built by William, son of Thomas Paty, who was the city's first architect and the first local to qualify at the Royal Academy. A large memorial to the city's merchant seaman is surrounded by seating. Past this on the quayside is a plaque recording the remains of a World War II bomb crater.

Continue to the pedestrianised end of King Street.

With your back to the water, on the left is the fine old pub, The Llandoger Trow. It is probably named after the town of Llandogo on the River Wye which once provided much of the city's food. It is 1 of 5 houses, but 2 were lost to World War II bombs. During the War of American Independence the Welsh boats known as trows were often raided by the pressgang. The mayor complained to the Admiralty that the boats were staying away and the people of Bristol were at risk of starvation.

Opposite this is The Old Duke, which dates from about 1750. An auction bill of 1805 gives its address as New King Street. The old King Street is now Merchant Street. At that time, the pub occupied a single room. For many years it has been a popular music venue, especially for jazz.

Buildings line the waterfront for some distance, so walk to the end of the pedestrianised area and turn left down Queen Charlotte Street.

The tall, ornate brick building on the left is The Granary, built in 1869 by Pontin & Gough. It was designed to be draughty and dark to preserve the grain and reduce the dust. It is 10 storeys high. For many years it was a rock venue, but has now been converted to apartments.

Continue straight ahead to Queen Square.

On your left as you reach the square is a house dating from about 1690. Its ornate shell hood over the door is typical of this time.

On the corner on the right is the site of the city's first mansion house, home to the mayor, again by Thomas Paty. It was here that the recorder Sir Charles Wetherall first took shelter when his arrival in the city triggered the 1831 riots. A young I K Brunel was a volunteer constable. Sir Charles claimed that the locals were not interested in politics, so they rioted to show him they were. He also opposed Catholic emancipation, so the Irish seamen and navvies in Marsh Street lodging houses also had grounds to protest. This house, like about a third of the square, was destroyed in the riots so is a rebuild.

After the riots, the square fell into decline as those with sufficient wealth moved to the healthier new streets and squares of Kingsdown and Clifton. On the east side, i.e., straight ahead, is the red brick Port Authority Office of 1885. It replaced properties long abandoned after the riots. It was built when the city took control of Avonmouth Docks. The Flemish Renaissance style is of its time, but is out of place here. It featured in the 2020 Agatha Christie miniseries 'The Pale Horse' starring Rufus Sewell.

Beyond it to the left is Redcliffe Swing Bridge, from 1942. Before this, travellers from the south used the ferry or detoured to Bristol Bridge. On the corner is the renovated 17th century Hole in the Wall pub. Facing The Grove is a porch with a small window. This was allegedly to watch out for the press gang which arrested men for the navy during wartime. In the 18th century it was known as The Coach and Horses.

Continue round the square to the right.

On the corner of Grove Avenue is a modern building. It bears a plaque recording that it was home to Woodes Rodgers, privateer and/or pirate. He captained the ship The Duke, which with its sister ship The Duchess made the most profitable expedition of the time. The genius navigator William Dampier was his navigator. and made maps that were used by James Cook. In 1709 they rescued the curmudgeonly Scottish castaway Alexander Selkirk from Juan Fernandez Island. Claims are made that his story inspired Daniel Defoe's 'Robinson Crusoe'. But there were many other castaways at the time, including, briefly, Dampier, and the novel was set in the Caribbean. Rogers became governor of the Bahamas in 1717 to suppress the last of the region's pirates. He died there in 1732.

Continue towards Princes Street.

On the far right corner is a badly damaged church, the Seamen's Mission of c.1880. It provided support for poor mariners who risked spending all their wages before shipping out again. The chapel was above. It was bombed in 1940 and very badly repaired. Its prolonged neglect is a disgrace, but has been rescued by a local pub.

Retrace your steps and turn right into Grove Avenue to cross at the lights.

From the water's edge are fine views of the floating harbour and St Mary Redcliffe. The Thekla boat is named after an obscure Greek goddess. It arrived here in 1982 as The Old Profanity Showboat by Kit Longfellow-Stanshall and her husband Viv Stanshall. Viv was a member of the 'Bonzo Dog Dooh Dah Band' and he narrated Mike Oldfield's album 'Tubular Bells' which began Richard Branson's Virgin empire. The boat has long been a local music venue. It is in the New Mud Dock which was built in the 1770s to increase quay space and protect boats from being torn from their moorings by the surging tides.

To the right, the Old Mud Dock was a graving dock for repairing boats. Beside this was the famous great crane built by engineer John Padmore who was also consulted on the crumbling archway of St Nicholas church. The crane was built on wooden pillars and goods were stored beneath for protection from the elements. Its image was featured on many maps.

Across the water is Merchants' Quay, a busy boat-building area in the 18th century. In the 1860s Brunel's Dock Railway was built from Temple Meads through Redcliffe Hill to reach the busy port area. Leading to it, to the right, is Princes Street Swing Bridge, originally a pedestrian toll bridge. It was rebuilt by the corporation in 1897 and operated by the radical new method of hydraulics. The city's first electric street lights were installed here and on Bathurst Wharf. This was probably to prevent people slipping into the harbour and drowning.

Follow the water's edge to the right to reach Princes Street.

The far side of the street was once lined with houses as grand as those on Queen Square. A few survive from the 1740s. Nicholas Pocock lived here at the end of the 18th century. He was a local sea captain who became a famous maritime artist. His work can be seen in the city museum.

In front of you is Bush House, a warehouse inspired by the Wool Hall of Thomas Street. It was built in 1830 as a warehouse for iron but later stored tea. In 1975 the far side of it became the pioneering modern arts venue, the Arnolfini. It had several previous addresses including Queen Square. The quayside there is a great place to watch the sun go down on a warm summer evening.

Cross Princes Street to the corner of the quay to see a statue of John Cabot gazing thoughtfully downstream. No contemporary images of him survive. This is the junction of the original route of the Avon with the 13th century diversion of the River Frome. Across the water is Lloyds Bank amphitheatre on the site of 19th century bonded tobacco warehouses. Along the waterside were Victorian warehouses where some locals recall banana boats docking. Most of the warehouses have been rebuilt as bars though further along to the right, the Watershed Arts Centre occupies a building by Edward Gabriel from 1894.

Follow the water's edge round to the right.

The pedestrian bridge, with 'wings' as counterbalances to allow it to be raised, is dedicated to Pero, a black slave and servant. He was brought from Nevis by the Pinney family. Their former home is now the Georgian House Museum on Great George Street.

In 1880 the River Frome, long an open sewer lined with traffic-choked streets, began to be covered over. This allowed Colston Avenue to be created in 1892, and in 1937 the final stretch from Baldwin Street was covered over.

Continue towards a lead statue of Neptune.

This is the oldest secular statue in the city. It has been moved so many times for road widening that locals joke he should be fitted with wheels. It was originally beside the Temple Pipe outlet. A plaque in the museum claims it was built to celebrate the defeat of the Spanish Armada in 1588, but it was cast by parishioner Mr Randal in 1723. It was at the bottom of Temple Street, then outside Dr White's almshouse. When Bath Street (yet another Paty project) was built in 1786 the Temple Market Cross was demolished and Neptune moved to Bear Lane.

He was originally brightly painted with his trident gilded. In 1793 the Chamberlain was expected for the opening of the rebuilt St Thomas' church, but the trident was still absent.

"A wag had climbed over the railings and placed a red herring in his uplifted hand making him look as though he had been carousing... and was bringing home a savoury morsel for his seedy godship's feast."

Victoria Street was ploughed through the southern parishes in 1845 during a frenzy of street improvements. The bridge was widened and Neptune was again moved to make way for traffic. He was "bronzed and burnished" and placed at the junction of Victoria and Temple Streets. In 1949 he was cleaned and moved to his present site on The Centre and given his granite base. In 1982 he was in a poor state so was repaired by a sculptor but this was difficult as he was filled with concrete.

Beyond him in a strange pose is a statue of Edward Burke, local MP from 1774 to 1780. His support for Irish trade instead of that of Bristol ensured he was not nominated again. He often had a yo-yo added to his outstretched hand when students had such things.

For a time this area was called Magpie Park after a short-lived newspaper published nearby. At the end of the park beyond the lights is the plinth which is all that remains of Edward Colston's statue. It was spectacularly toppled on 7 June 2020 during protests inspired by the Black Lives Matter campaign.

It is by John Cassidy, of 1895, an early bronze piece of art nouveau. Pevsner's architectural guide of 2004 is hardly a radical publication, but it claimed "suggestions that the statue be removed … have not been followed". On the corners of the plinth are large ugly fish, claimed to be the merchant's emblem of dolphins. They could be the barbel fish on the Colston family's coat of arms, or perhaps cod, a major part of the city's international trade.

Beyond this is a Grade II listed fountain with the city's coat of arms, made of pink and grey granite. It was built in 1901 to commemorate the promoters of the popular Industrial and Fine Art Exhibition of 1892–3. It raised funds of £2,200 for 5 Bristol medical charities. One promoter was the local printer and publisher J W Arrowsmith who was also the major promoter of the Colston statue.

Beyond this is the Cenotaph of 1932, by a local firm based on a Luytens design, the last of its kind to be built. The delays were the result of the popular local tradition of arguing.

To the left along the roadside is a horse trough dedicated to animal-loving Captain Nicholetts, RN who died in 1908. He had supervised the 'Formidable', run by the Bristol Training Ship Association. The association's aim was to reclaim "destitute and neglected boys from the haunts of ignorance, wretchedness and vices". Sending boys to sea had long been a popular way to provide cheap labour for the navy and merchant shipping. It also prevented young men from turning to crime or needing parish poor relief.

To the right, leading off The Centre is the church of St Stephen's. The church is often open to the public and is popular with people researching family history. It has a cafe and a quiet garden. See its website for opening times.

This church is unusual for many reasons. The original Norman church was established by a cell from Glastonbury Abbey. This was beyond the town walls and the River Frome before the 13th century. The new course of the river separated it from St Augustines Abbey, creating its own parish. The church was rebuilt c.1470 funded by Glastonbury Abbey. Its soaring four-tiered Somerset tower was funded by merchant John Shipward, who also left land to support the poor, and the fraternity of St Clements which evolved into the Merchant Venturers. It was never designed for chapel ceremonies or congregational worship. The merchant community invoked help from saints including Katherine, James, and John the Baptist. With between 5 and 9 chantry chapels, it was a wealthy prayer factory. At the Reformation it owned 1,000 ounces of silver plate which allowed the city to buy its churches from the Crown. This is why the parish churches remained independent. The only local record of the Great Storm of 27 November 1703 tells that all 3 battlements and the clock fell through the roof of the nave, and the whole length of Temple Street was navigable by boat. The storm caused massive damage across northern Europe, drowning all the marsh country on both sides of the Severn. All the warehouses and cellars were flooded so the merchants suffered huge losses. Boats were rowed along Temple Street, and some were sent from the city to rescue many people who were found in trees etc.

In 1733 the church was wainscotted and provided with new pews, all in the newly fashionable Caribbean wood, mahogany.

Several ancient tombs, including that of Edmund Blanket and his wife, are below the current floor level. This proves the existence of the previous church. St Stephen's has a sword rest from the blitzed St Nicholas church, and an ornate chair made from a previous pulpit. The parish became home to many wealthy Huguenots. The most famous was Maryanne Peloquin whose plain monument survives. She was the last of her family and donated her home on Queen Square to become a parsonage. In 1779 she bequeathed vast sums to the corporation for distribution, including £5,000 to the Infirmary and £15,200, the interest from which was to support 38 each of men and women across the city. £2,500 was left for poor lying-in women and 20 poor single women or widows and 10 poor men of the parish. This added up to a total of £19,000. Josiah Tucker was a famous, busy and sociable 18th century incumbent. He promoted the abolition of slavery and was friends with John Newton of 'Amazing Grace' fame, and Hannah More.

Most relevant to this walk is the coloured monument to Martin

Pring. He sailed to Cape Cod in 1603, a captain aged only 23, under license from Raleigh. Pring was a member of the Merchant Venturers, who funded the expedition. He explored and mapped the area later settled by the Pilgrim Fathers, and planted crops to establish their suitability for the region. He later sailed to the Far East, paving the way for the East India Company's trading posts. He died in 1626.

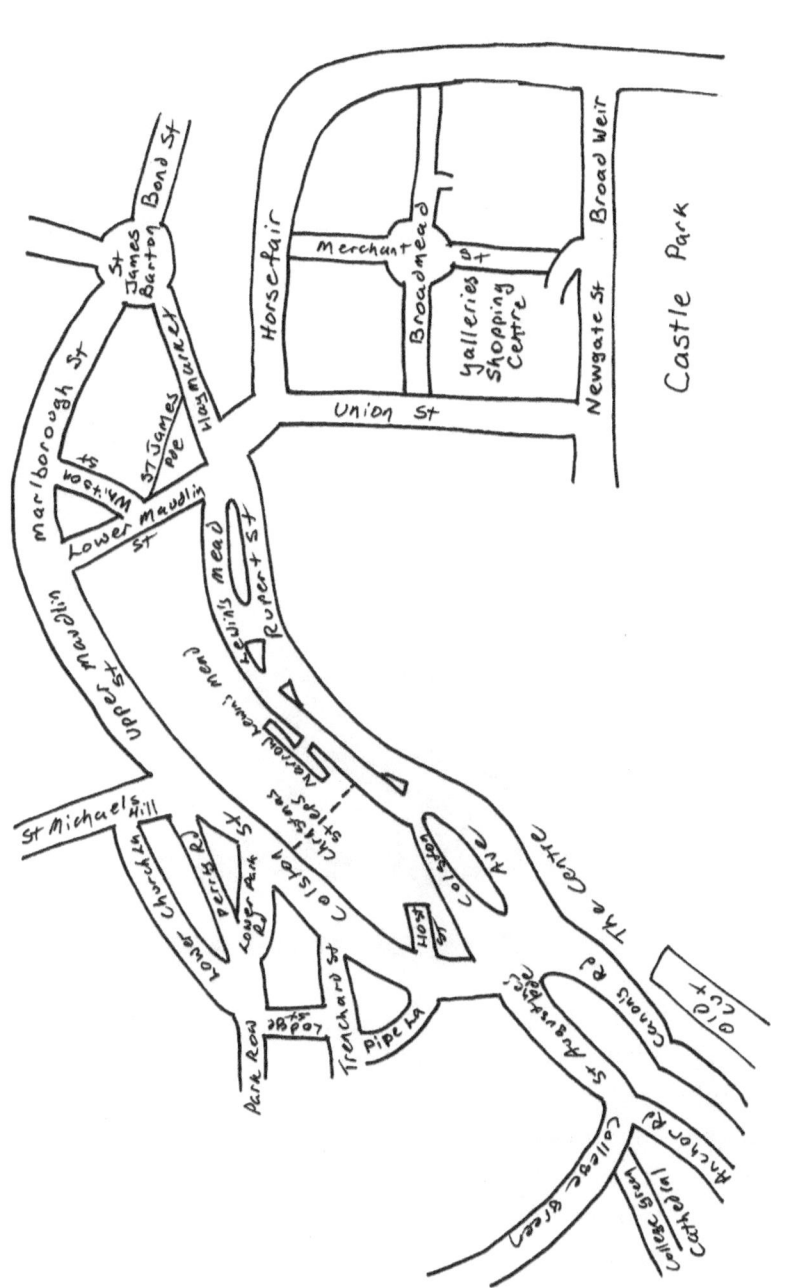

SIX

God's Many Houses

Start: Quakers' Friars
End: Colston Parade, city centre
Length: Approx. 1.75km /1.25 miles
Route: Mixture of pedestrianised and mixed use streets. Steep slopes up and down, including some steps.
Public transport: Any buses to city centre/Broadmead
PREAMBLE
Bristol Cathedral was founded in 1140 as the Abbey of St Augustine by Robert Fitzharding, later the first Lord Berkeley. But it had no

important relics to attract pilgrims and their funds, so struggled to fund long term expenditure such as building projects. It was being rebuilt at the time of the Reformation, so it did not reach its present form until the nineteenth century. It became a cathedral at The Reformation, which made Bristol a city.

Thomas Howell was bishop during the Civil War. But Parliamentarians claimed to have bought his house and removed lead from its roof whilst his wife was expecting the latest of their many children. She died from the shock. Their house was converted to a brewhouse and the strain of trying to recover it killed the bishop. The bishopric was empty for fourteen years until Gilbert Ironside was elected in 1660. He had enough private income to restore the Bishop's palace.

Joseph Butler was bishop from 1738. In 1744 he rebuilt the ruinous palace at his own expense and where he lived in the summer.

Mary Robinson was born there in 1758. After a bad marriage she was forced to earn her own living so became an actress. She became famous for her role as Perdita in Shakespeare's 'A Winter's Tale'. She became disgraced for having an affair with the Prince of Wales, and a miscarriage left her wheelchair bound so she supported herself as a poet and novelist, focusing on women's rights.

But the bishopric was poorly paid and called 'the Cinderella of all Sees'. It seldom attracted men of talent; most used the post as a stepping stone to more lucrative positions. Only Bishop Secker became Archbishop of Canterbury. Bishop Butler was responsible for the completion of the cathedral. One of the towers is dedicated to him, the other to Edward Colston. But it was outside the old city, so it was not supported by locals.

By contrast, the many well-maintained parish churches in the city have been highly praised for their construction and support. But in the 18th century many wealthy parishioners left the decaying central area. This meant some parishes became too small to support themselves. Several churches were altered or demolished for road widening while the rest were repaired and rebuilt. In an age when clerics were often absentee, many in Bristol were noted for being conscientious and lived locally.

But as the city expanded into new suburbs from the seventeenth century, new church foundations failed to follow their congregations. The only new parishes were St Paul's, carved out of the crowded industrial parish of St James, and St George's, which was carved out of the huge rural parish of St Phillip and Jacob that stretched halfway to Bath. This region was home to many poor miners who came to the city to riot over high food prices. The lack of gentry meant there was a lack of support for the many parish poor. John Wesley had pioneered evangelising there and encouraged middle class settlers.

To the north, Redland chapel was built by the owners of Redland House, John and Martha Cossins. It is unclear why it took decades to become licensed as the parish church.

Dowry Square Chapel served visitors to the spa at Hotwells before it was bombed in World War II. The Strangers' Burial Ground survives off Jacob's Wells Road.

The site of St George's Brandon Hill on Great George Street began as an overflow graveyard for St Augustine-the-Less in the centre, now replaced by the Royal Hotel. The church was built by Sir Robert Smirke as a chapel of ease to St Augustine's in 1821–3. The design was used at St James in Hackney. It is surrounded by expensive late 18th and early 19th century housing. But the parish also included the docks so it had a large population of working people and the poor. It was the first of the city's 8 poor parishes funded by the government to celebrate victory over the French, hence its dedication to St George. When Queen Elizabeth Hospital moved to Jacobs Wells Road in 1847, it became the school's place of worship. Several pupils are commemorated there, including the architect William Paty. He was last member of the family business, and his memorial is in the porch.

Post-war depopulation eventually made the church redundant in 1984. But the BBC discovered its near-perfect acoustics so they converted it to a concert hall in 1985. Since 1999 it has been St Georges Brandon Hill, one of the city's most popular venues. During its 2020 expansion to create a cafe and other facilities, the former graveyard was excavated. It had been laid out on 3 levels, with the poor at the bottom. Some of the bones show knife marks. It seems they were used by students from the Royal Infirmary to practice their surgical skills.

After the Blitz, the council encouraged an exodus from the old city. This allowed the long-planned establishment of department stores in the centre. New estates were built in the suburbs and most of the parishes followed their flocks outward. But the new estates failed to flourish as there was little support and infrastructure. Complaints were made that people could not afford the bus fairs to the centre so were excluded from work there. In 1940 St Mary-le-Port's congregation moved to St John-on-the-Wall until their declining numbers led to its closure in 1984. The small group remaining moved to the chapel of Foster's Almshouse at the top of Christmas Steps. No longer listed as members of the Anglican Church, some joined the Free Presbyterians of Ulster at Horfield. St John's church is now in the care of the Churches Conservation Trust.

The early history of religious houses and faith groups is described in the introduction to this book. The history of Bristol's first parish churches can be found in Walks nos. 1 and 2. This walk takes in many churches in the central and northern area of the old city and suburbs.

THE AMBLE

Start in the centre of Quakers' Friars in Cabot Circus shopping centre. The development was to be named the Merchants Quarter, but this was opposed due to the alleged association with the slave trade. Much of this site was built by the Dominicans, or Black Friars, named after the colour of their habits. They were funded by begging for alms rather than by wealthy patrons, so their buildings were functional rather than ornate. It had a church, orchards, gardens and beehives alongside the banks of the River Frome which separated them from the castle. They probably sold produce for extra income. The parts that have survived the Reformation were mostly domestic buildings. They became halls for the cutlers' and bakers' guilds. The Bakers' Hall was possibly the friars' infirmary of c.1230.

Quakers, like other non-Anglican groups, were excluded from trading in the city, as they refused to take the Oath of Supremacy. They settled here, beyond the city's walls. They had a school from

1668 and a meeting house from 1670, where William Penn was married. But it became ruinous so it was rebuilt in 1743 by George Tully, who may have been a Quaker, with stonework by Thomas Paty. For many years after the war it was the local registry office, surrounded by car parking, but it is now a restaurant. By the 1970s the region was described by Pevsner as "Bristol's greatest planning failure of the 1950s". Plenty of other developments in the city provided stiff competition for that title.

Take the northern exit from the area (furthest from Castle Park). Turn left into Broadmead, right into Merchant Street, then left into The Horsefair to Wesley's New Room on the left.

John Wesley was an Oxford-educated Anglican cleric. With his brother Charles, and George Whitfield, he tried to reform the Anglican church via a system they developed called the Method. They promoted the concept that salvation is available to all, but were eventually forced to form a separate organisation. John built his first meeting house here in 1739. Many local sources claim it was set well back from the road to try to keep it secret. A similar claim is made for the Theatre Royal, as if crowds of people would not be noticed. The arrangement was to save money. Property rents were based on the width of street frontages which were in demand for shops.

As the name suggests, the New Room was not a church but a meeting place where the poor could come for help. There was upstairs accommodation for Wesley and travelling ministers as well as meeting and work rooms. Wesley's small bedroom survives. It shows the window shelf where he wrote his many sermons to maximise the light. He was still in demand as a preacher in parish churches for some years. The old building soon became too small and was falling down so the present building dates from 1748. The preaching desk is lit by a lantern-style window. The design impressed Wesley on passenger ships when he crossed the Atlantic. The pillars are believed to be ships' masts. The building was paid for by forming groups dedicated to raising funds, a precursor of microcredit. It was painted cornflower and white but has now been restored to its original colour of 'drab'.

When Wesley died, there was no charismatic or powerful replacement. The Methodists splintered into smaller groups. From 1808 to 1929 the building was home to Welsh Methodists. It then returned to the Wesleyans and was restored the following year. The building houses a museum, hosts performances, and of course there is a cafe.

Return to The Horsefair and turn left into Union Street. Its name commemorates England's union with Scotland in 1707. About halfway along is the entrance to the Baptist church of 1969. From across the street, you can see a series of doves descending on the upper facade of the building. Baptists have worshipped on this site since 1671. The group opposed the African slave trade and their ministers in the Caribbean were often harassed by plantation owners. The old church of 1815 was demolished after World War II, but some stained glass has been preserved. Most city churches followed their congregations to the new suburbs after the war. But the Baptists stayed to minister to the poor. When the Broadmead area was redeveloped, the church sold the ground floor and built the present church upstairs in 1969.

Retrace your steps down Union Street and cross the Haymarket to the disused churchyard of St James', now a public park.

Like many others, the overcrowded churchyard was closed under the 1854 Health in Towns Act. It was later landscaped as part of its conversion to a public park, with the area on the left becoming a paved children's play area. It was in the Wesley's parish, and a monument to John's brother Charles stands to the right. The huge annual St James' Fair was held here and on surrounding streets from 1238 till 1838 when shopping habits changed. It attracted traders with a year's worth of goods from Wales, Ireland, London, the Midlands and even Russia. Barbary pirates sometimes seized ships carrying traders on their way to the fair in the Bristol Channel.

On the far side and to the right on St James Parade is a small church that was built for Scottish Presbyterians in 1858 which had a spire. It has now been converted to offices. There is also a cafe run by St James Priory which has an entrance to the church.

Follow the path to your left to reach Lower Maudlin Street.

This street was named after the St Augustinian nunnery of the Magdalenes, or White Ladies. Their house was at the base of St Michael's Hill which was funded by lands extending from this area as far as what is now Clifton Down Shopping Centre. The road named after them forms the eastern boundary of Clifton which is widely believed to suggest links with the slave trade. But this would be a tautology as all 'ladies' in those days were white, as the houses were run by aristocrats. The name comes from the fact that they wore white robes.

On the right corner of the street is the White Hart Inn, an ancient hostelry where visitors to the priory were said to have found lodgings. It was probably used by travellers arriving after the town gates had closed at night.

Continue past the inn and turn right into Whitson Street, named after the great medieval benefactor and magnate John Whitson. Turn right at the main entrance to St James' Priory.

It was founded by Robert Earl of Gloucester in the 12th century as a cell of Tewkesbury Abbey and received land rents from several parishes in the city. The nave became the parish church in 1374 making it one of the oldest buildings in the city. It was home to many of Bristol's finest families, and an impressive selection of distinctive memorials survive. The front is a strange mix of local rubble stone with carved limestone above. It was a wealthy house, funded by extensive lands, and donations from many donors, but especially the annual St James' Fair and taxes on wine. The site was divided in 1672 and much of it redeveloped. It was a large house and some of its ruins survived until the 1780s.

The parish church houses an unusual corbel on the roof: half woman, half pig. There is a bust by locally born E.H. Bailey, or Baily, silversmith to Queen Victoria. From the mid-14th century it was the parish church for one of the city's most densely populated areas. The crypt was used by the Medieval Guild of the Holy Cross, a charity. For many years it was home to the Roman Catholic charity Little Brothers of Nazareth who helped the local poor. The church was then only open to the public on the annual Doors Open Day. It is now a

Catholic church, open to the public as a quiet space for prayer Mondays to Fridays, 10–5, but please check their website to confirm times.

St James' parish was the site of 7 almshouses, and the Royal Infirmary was founded in 1760, possibly the first in the country. But it has been scandalously demolished for yet another concrete and glass carbuncle of student housing. In the 1770s there was also the city's first Roman Catholic chapel and seven Protestant dissenting chapels including Whitfield's tabernacle, houses of Moravians, Quakers and Presbyterians.

Return to Lower Maudlin Street.

Uphill, is the Eye Hospital founded by Unitarian minister Dr Lant Carpenter. It has some fine brick relief sculptures by Walter Ritchie. of 1986, at the time believed to be the largest hand-carved brick sculpture in the world. In the 18th century, this was the site of the Moravian chapel and graveyard. The Moravians were often linked with the Methodists. The local group was founded by hymn writer John Cennick who also founded a group at Kingswood in 1742. Many members were Europeans and some Welsh, often tradespeople from the lower middle class. Their communities were dispersed across many areas of the globe and their newsletters were second only to The Bible in readership.

Turn left down Lower Maudlin Street, then turn right into Lewins Mead.

Several tower blocks loom above. Lewin was probably a Saxon, the son of Aelric, a major local figure. He was linked to both the Fitzharding interests and was chamberlain to the Earl of Gloucester's household. He held land in the area, and also Bedminster, Redcliffe, Keynsham, Dundry and near Glastonbury. Some land rents were paid in eels and salmon, which suggests both were found in the Frome at the time.

The tower blocks are on the former sites of the Greyfriars and Whitefriars religious houses beside the Frome. They were destroyed and their materials sold in the Reformation. The overhead walkways are relics of the brave new metropolis. They date from the 1960s when town planners became drunk on American modernism and the ideas of Le Corbusier, whose nephew lived in the city. Pedestrians were relegated to walkways above the traffic. They created a series of wind tunnels and a major site for graffiti art. The council wanted to move all housing out of the centre to new estates, leaving the centre for business. They tore apart close communities, failed to provide support and many were too poor to pay for bus fares to the centre for work. Many are still struggling.

Continue to the neglected Lewins Mead Chapel.

The first modern building on this site was a chapel for Presbyterians, from 1694. It became Unitarian by the 1780s under J.P. Estlin who ran a respected school upstairs. The present building of 1787–91 was designed by William Blackburn, a rare commission for a non-local. He specialised in prisons, including the one at Lawford's Gate which was destroyed in the 1831 riots. His hallmark was to decorate them with manacles mimicking Roman garlands. This was the church of numerous alderman and mayors by the 1780s. For many years it worked with the older chapel at Tucker Street which moved to Bridge Street, then to Clifton Down.

Adjoining this is the early 18th century former sugar house, i.e., refinery. As these establishments boiled the sugar night and day, most were destroyed by fires, so this is a rare survivor. It is now a hotel and restaurant.

Go past a statue of the 'Cloaked Horseman' by David Backhouse, erected in 1984. Continue beneath a modern covered walkway to the ancient gateway on the right.

This was St Bartholomew's Hospital, founded c.1230–40. It was a small, mixed community of men and women. But it was poorly funded by the de la Warr family who remained its patrons until it was dissolved by Henry VIII in 1532. It began as a priory, and evolved into a hospital for the poor. Its quadrangular buildings became home to Bristol Grammar School, funded by the Thorne family to produce a new, literate merchant class. The tragic poet Thomas Chatterton was a student there. Some people also left legacies in their wills to train scholars to study at Oxford to become clerics. It had a good playground and in 1759–60 hundreds of pounds were spent on improvements. But in 1764 Rev. Charles Lee became headmaster and married the daughter of Alderman Dampier. Apparently the alderman wanted a more pleasant home for his daughter to live, so arranged for the grammar school to swap with Queen Elizabeth Hospital on College Green. This was despite QEH having been granted the site forever, and had been greatly improved at the start of the century. After 1847 it was adapted for housing and a printer was located there.

A defaced medieval statue of the Virgin and child and a fine archway survive. The former St Bartholomew's Hospital site was previously open to the public, and the archaeological remains, with information boards, could be viewed. It is now owned by people who apparently have no knowledge of its history, and there is no public access.

Continue past this gated entrance and a famous fish and chip shop to turn right and climb Christmas Steps.

This is one of the few places where the old city is clearly visible, and it is home to some interesting shops and cafes. Most buildings date from the 17th century. Unbelievably, this steep pedestrian way was once the main road to Wales. But it must have been a major cause of slips and falls in bad weather. Complaints were often made of the damage caused to the road surface by packhorses, so whirligigs were built to stop them passing. It acquired steps in 1669.

It was originally known as Knifesmith Street, but by 1673 it was Queen Street. At the bottom, access to the River Frome made it a popular place for washing laundry. At the top on the left is the Chapel of the Three Kings of Cologne, or Three Wise Men. This is the only such dedication in this country. It is part of the almshouse founded by merchant John Foster in 1483. It was rebuilt in a fantastic French chateau style by Foster & Wood from 1861. It is of course now in private ownership as it was deemed unsafe for old people.

At the top of Christmas Steps, cross Colston Street and take another flight of steps almost directly opposite. Cross Perry Road at the traffic lights.

St Michael's Hill was the continuation of the main road to Wales. The King David Hotel on the right corner is an 1891 rebuild of a much older inn. The name may be a post-Reformation secularising of

St David, patron saint of Wales. Uphill on the right was the Magdalene, Carmelite, or White Ladies nunnery mentioned earlier. Its remains were still shown on Horfield Road on the 1901 Ordnance Survey map. The order here was funded by rents from lands which extended to the present Clifton Down Shopping Centre, hence the name Whiteladies Road. Foundations of male clerics raised funds from holding church services, especially prayers for the dead, but women had no such resources. Claims that the term was linked to slavery ignore the fact that this would be a tautology.

Cross at the traffic lights and turn left to take the steps up to Church Road.

Towering above you is the former parish church of St Michael Without. It was founded in 1193 and rebuilt in the 15th century to serve the merchants settling on the slope outside the festering city. At the Dissolution of the Monasteries it was sold to Henry Brayne Esq who obtained several other churches in Bristol, for £676 7s 6d. In 1627 Bristol corporation purchased the church. In 1739 its 6 bells were installed, paid by a subscription and a local rate. But by the middle of the 18th century the structure was decayed as the population of the parish expanding. The graveyard walls had repeatedly collapsed, spreading 'mould' onto the road. 1774 Thomas Paty was employed to build a new, larger edifice after falling masonry almost killed several people. The corporation gave £300 and the Merchant Venturers £150. Queen Anne's bounty also contributed, showing the parish was poor. Many monuments were destroyed by the rebuilding.

The current church has been condemned as dull, and further evidence of Paty's limited skill as an architect, but the building survives. The parish records reveal the horrors of churchwardens with no knowledge of the building profession. They kept demanding changes while refusing to fund them. Paty must have had the patience of a saint, as he probably lost money on the project. Post war migration to the outer suburbs emptied the parish and the church was deconsecrated in 1999, then damaged by fire. It is now a community and creative space called The Mount Without

To the left up Church Lane is the Gothic style rectory which was rebuilt at the same time.

A room from the previous rectory with fine linenfold wainscotting can be seen at the Red Lodge Museum if it is open.

Turn left along Church Lane and then right into Perry Road.

A short distance further along, on the uphill side of Perry Road, is the Orthodox synagogue. It is behind ornate iron gates and a formidable rank of steps and CCTV. It was opened in 1871 on part of a site briefly owned by a French Catholic sisterhood, the Little Sisters of the Poor. When the road was widened, they moved to a larger site on Clifton Down after the Bridge Street Chapel congregation died out.

Cross Park Row at the pedestrian lights to the Red Lodge.

This was built c.1577–85 on the site of the former Carmelite friary. It was demolished in 1568 to make way for a lodge to the Great House.

Elizabeth I stayed at the Great House on her visit to the city. But it decayed and eventually became a sugar house. It was rebuilt as the first Colston school, then replaced with the first Colston Hall in 1863. The site is now the Beacon arts centre. If it ever opens.

From 1854 the lodge was home to Mary Carpenter's Female Reformatory, funded by Lady Byron. It is now a city museum, with free entry.

In the garden is a huge, weathered statue of the former attorney general and recorder, Sir Charles Weatherall. His arrival in the city triggered the 1831 riots. Also in the garden is the 'wigwam' of the Bristol Savages. They were a group of artists, writers and musicians who began to meet socially in 1894. From 1907 they met at Brandon Cottage at no.2 Brandon Steep. In 1917 they bought the Red Lodge and donated it to the city to become a museum. Following the Colston riots this all male group has been renamed 'Bristol 1904 Arts' and now more open to the membership of women.

Turn down Lodge Street beside the museum. Turn left at the bottom into Trenchard Street.

On the left the large Georgian Gothic building is the former St

Joseph's Chapel of 1790. It was the first Roman Catholic chapel to be built in Bristol. The Irish giant Patrick O'Brien was buried here under several feet of concrete to prevent his skeleton being dug up and toured as a freak show. For a time it was a boy's school, but is now owned by the Church of England.

At the end of Trenchard Street, cross Colston Street, and take Zed Alley to the left of the Gloucester Sports Club. Cross over Host Street, where there are several ancient warehouses on the cobbled street, to the busy Colston Parade on The Centre.

St Mary-on-the-Quay is the only temple-style church in central Bristol. It was built in 1839 by Irvingites, or Catholic Apostolics. They moved to the smaller church on Elmdale Road off the top of Park Street and in 1871 sold their original church to the Jesuits. In 1878 the poet Gerald Manly Hopkins served as priest for a year.

On the front buttress is a plaque to parishioners who died in World War I. The first name is that of G. Archer Shee. He was a cadet at Osborne Naval College on the Isle of Wight who was accused of theft. But his father, the manager of the local Bank of England branch, defended him. The case became such a cause celebré that Terence Rattigan immortalised it in his play 'The Winslow Boy'. It has been filmed several times, most recently in 1999.

Across the centre can be seen the soaring tower of St Stephen's church. It is described at the end of walk no. 5, Follow the Tide. It is worth a visit and it has a fine cafe and garden.

Stay on this side of The Centre, cross Colston Street and veer up the hill to College Green.

Facing the middle of the green is St Mark's Chapel. The chapel is unique as it has never been a parish church. It has had a varied history since Maurice Berkeley de Gaunt built a hospital on the site in 1229 for a chaplain to care for 100 poor people each day. It was funded by a local manor and several mills and supervised by St Augustine's canons. But on his death, Berkeley's nephew Robert de Gournay converted it to a house for a master or prior, and 3 chaplains, to support the local poor. It was dedicated to the Virgin and St Mark and known as St Mark's Hospital. It expanded to include a small priory. Its master and 3 priests encouraged useful pastimes including 'the mechanic arts'. Like many sites in the city, this has a historic resonance. It is at – or near – the former Merchant Venturers Technical College which took up the side of Unity Street. The organisation's coat of arms is on the corner building's pediment.

Gaunt's nephew Robert de Gournay converted it into the Gaunt's Hospital and included the Poyntz chantry chapel of 1523. It funded a hospital or guesthouse for well-born ladies or gentry who prayed for the souls of the donors. It also included a small almshouse with a single chaplain feeding 100 poor people.

William Barratt describes a dispute between St Marks and William Chew, vicar of St Augustine-the-less in 1426. Having burials of the rich and powerful in their parish helped attract funds. The vicar of St Augustines was accused of burying 2 people who lived in the precincts of St Mark's and were buried 'unjustly' in the churchyard of St Augustines. Their bodies were ordered to be dug up and reinterred with full rituals to the Hospital of St Mark.

In October 1822 a body was stolen from the same St Augustine's graveyard and delivered to the dissection room of several surgeons in the Cathedral precincts. But an argument drew the attention of a crowd, but it seems no action was taken.

In 1541 the corporation bought the property to become the only church owned by a local authority. From the late 17th century the church was a Huguenot chapel but since 1722 it has been the Lord Mayor's Chapel. Its entrance was round the side. The original facade was moved to become a folly in a private garden at Henbury. It has a wonderful array of old tombs. Its stained glass is described by Pevsner as being of remarkable quality and quantity. Much of it is from Fonthill, including a window by Benjamin West. was mostly purchased in 1823. It is often open to the public and sometimes has concerts. It is now managed by the Cathedral, and charges for entry.

Cross College Green to Bristol Cathedral.

This was an Augustinian abbey founded c.1140 by Robert Fitzharding, the first Lord Beaufort. It was well supplied with lands for its upkeep. But it was unusual in having no famous relics to attract pilgrims. This limited its ability to fund large-scale improvements or to attract high quality bishops. It was often used as a stepping stone to better-funded posts. It was being rebuilt when Henry VIII closed the monasteries, so in 1542 it became one of 6 new dioceses. With Gloucester, it was in the diocese of Worcester, so it has always been separate from the main city. Dean Gilbert Elliot campaigned to enlarge and complete it. But in 1860–1 G G Scott had ordered much destruction of the interior which was widely criticised. Funds were raised for the work to be completed by G E Street which was achieved in 1877. The towers were then completed in 1887–8. It is mostly faced with Dundry stone. It is usually open and the chapter house in particular is worth a visit.

In the 18th century it was a popular venue for concerts, especially Handel's Messiah. It serves the adjoining Cathedral School, and hosts services and other events. The cathedral has some fine monuments, but few are of locals. Its crossing has a poets corner to commemorate many of the great and the good. Some of them were not Anglicans, such as the Unitarian reformer Mary Carpenter. Nearby is a plaque to Sydney Smith who preached in support of Catholic toleration and political reform. The Lady Chapel has some extraordinary 12th century carvings, including what seem to be green animals, as well as a green man. Past the crossing on the left is a heartbreaking monument to William Mason's wife Mary, one of many who died of tuberculosis after seeking a cure at the Hotwells. The final 4 lines were by Thomas Day, the abolitionist poet. Your heart will melt on reading it. He survived her by decades but never remarried.

At the end of the north aisle in the mariners' chapel is a partly obscured memorial to the great promotor of exploration, the prebend in 1585–1616 Richard Hakluyt, erected in the early 9th century as he is buried in Westminster Abbey. Nearby is a bust of locally born Poet Laureate Robert Southey. In the north choir is a large memorial to the much-loved theatre manager William Powell. As he lay dying at home in King Street, the roadway outside was covered in straw to reduce the noise.

In the cloister, memorials include some who returned from the

West Indies for their health but died at the Hotwells spa. The cathedral profited from many of their burials and are now investigating these links. The large memorial to Elizabeth Draper, allegedly Sterne's Eliza, is by John Bacon. The cathedral's role in the city over the years is hard to fathom as it was never a parish church. That role was served by St Augustine-the-Less. After World War II, the fall in the local population made that church redundant, so it was demolished. Its site is now the Royal Hotel. Thomas Paty's family produced some of the memorials here and across the region and in the West Indies. He was buried in St Augustine-the-Less. The memorial to his eldest son, William is in the porch of its daughter church, St George's Brandon Hill.

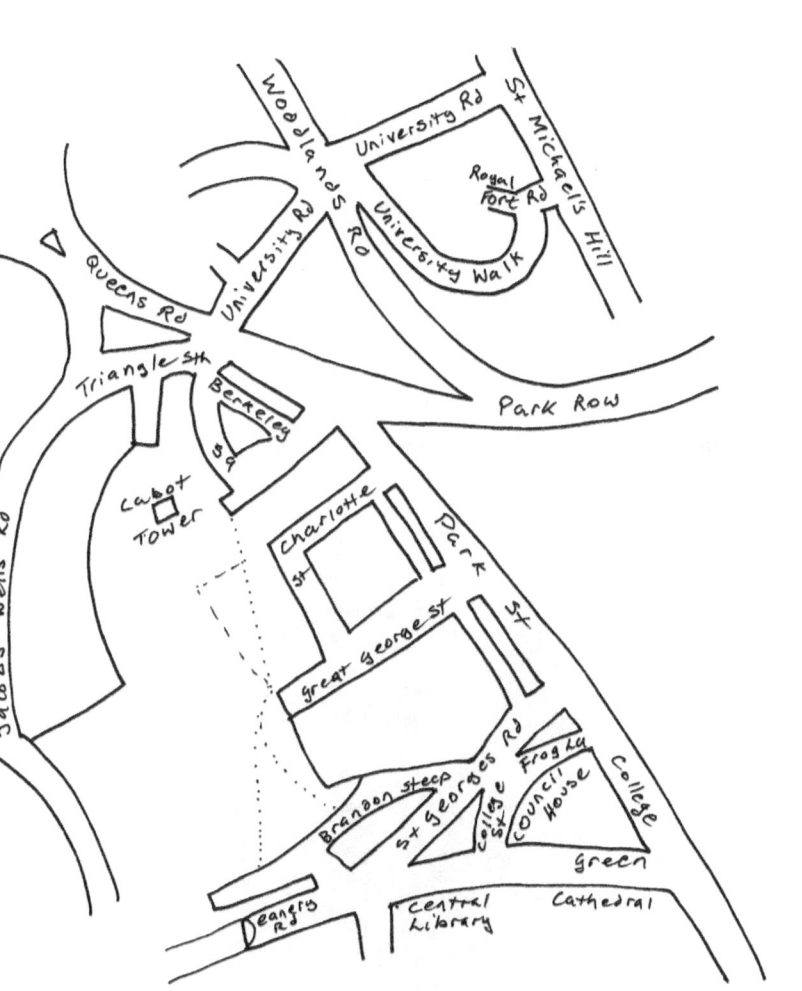

SEVEN

Georgian Heights & Victorian Landmarks

Start: Central Library, College Green
End: Tyndalls Park, University Precinct
Length: Approx. 1.5 km/1 mile

Route: Mostly quiet streets and parks. Overall climbing steeply uphill, no steps

Public Transport: Any buses to city centre /College Green. Return from top of Park Street.

PREAMBLE

This walk begins at the Central Library. It is arguably the city's finest building, as it blends modern architecture with Tudor elements to echo the adjoining cathedral gateway. The walk winds up Brandon Hill past Georgian houses and Victorian landmarks to the heights of Tyndall's Park, giving wonderful views of the city. On the highest point is Royal Fort House, built by the Tyndall family of bankers, which is now part of the university.

When Defoe visited Bristol he complained that the citizens refused to move beyond the city walls. But following the Civil War the walls became redundant for defence. Wealthy Bristolians then fled the crowded, unhealthy centre. The fine new houses on Queen Square set high standards for later developments. Tradesmen built workshops lining the road to Wales on St Michael's Hill, and further out the wealthy built summer houses. By the mid-eighteenth century, buildings were appearing round the base of Brandon Hill. This park was given to the Corporation of Bristol by the Earl of Gloucester in 1174. In 1533 Bristol Corporation confirmed it as a public open space, possibly the oldest in the country. The hill was topped by a windmill in the seventeenth century. Warning beacons and celebratory bonfires were lit there. It also saw at least one execution, rowdy meetings by Chartists and other protesters, and much carpet banging. Complaints were made about the laundresses ploughing up College Green with their sledges to take their clothes to dry on the hill.

It has fine views and a nature reserve. Cabot Tower was built in the 1890s to celebrate the 400th anniversary of Cabot reaching Newfoundland and was opened by the Canadian Ambassador. It was designed by W V Gough, a Bristolian who had settled in Canada.

Park Street was laid out through Bullock's Park. Fine merchants' houses appeared in speculative new developments such as Great George Street and Charlotte Square. Many were designed by various members of the Paty family, especially the sculptor and architect Thomas.

The 19th century was the great age of public buildings, often funded by wealthy industrialist and benefactors. Like Bath, Bristol is unusual in still having no town hall. The Guildhall and the twice burnt down Colston Hall were used for large gatherings. By the early 20th century Bristol had acquired a philosophical institution-cum-Museum, art gallery, university and central library, all of which showed the city's cultural aspirations. Many were funded by Nonconformists, and none by the corporation.

THE AMBLE

Start the walk at the Central Library on College Green.

The old library on King Street became the private Library Society in the 1770s. It was reclaimed for the public after a campaign in the 1870s. But the site was cramped and unable to expand to cope with the increasing public demand. In 1899 the retired banker and antiquarian Vincent Stuckey Lean bequeathed his book collection of three thousand volumes and a sum of £50,000 pounds to establish a new public library.

It opened 7 years later. The architect Charles Holden was only 27 when he won the competition to design the building, which has a classical interior of marble and teak. Its neo-Tudor exterior harmonises with the nearby cathedral. Pevsner praised its modernism and placed it alongside the much better known Glasgow School of Art. Carvings of literary greats such as Chaucer and St Augustine are on the facade. It was extended in 1968. The upstairs reference section includes the reading room from the old library. Its ornate overmantel is in the style of Grinling Gibbons. It may have been carved by local sculptor and architect Thomas Paty whose marble memorials can be seen in churches across the city and in Gloucestershire.

Mary Robinson was born in 1756 in the nearby Minster House. Like Thomas Chatterton in Redcliffe, she played in the cathedral ruins and was influenced by their history. She was educated at Hannah More's school on Park Street, but after marrying badly, she turned to the stage to survive. She was famous for the role of 'Perdita' in Shakespeare's "A Winter's Tale' and was a friend of Georgiana, Duchess of Devonshire. But she caused a scandal as a mistress of the future King George IV. She became paralysed but adapted to gain fame as a poet and playwright. She deserves a Blue Plaque here, but the library building is listed inside and out.

Outside is the 1997 statue to Calcutta's education and cultural reformer Raja Rammohun Roy who died on a visit to the region in 1843. His early death prevented him from achieving his full potential and fame. His huge ornate tomb is a feature of Arnos Vale Cemetery.

Cross the road outside the library and follow College Street behind the Council House.

Dominating the left side of St Georges Road is Brunel House. R.S. Pope built it to Brunel's designs in the Greek revival style as the Great Western Hotel. It was for travellers from London on the Great Western Railway who were waiting to embark on the SS Great Britain. It then because was Bristol City Council offices but is now yet more student accommodation. Through the coach entrance is a space once used for the horse bazaar. In the courtyard is the Stephen Joyce sculpture Horse and Man of 1984. It can be seen through closed gates. The cliff face behind it shows it was originally used as a quarry for local building stone. This was Bullock's Park. With Great George Street, it was laid out for development in 1770, and other streets followed up the hill.

Follow St Georges' Road to the right, up the slope to Park Street.

On the uphill corner is the Freemasons' Hall which is unique as the meeting place for all the local lodges. It was bombed in the war and the interior has been completely rebuilt. Its predecessor was the Philosophical Institution, a pioneering museum, library and place for public lectures. The first curator was the father of the painter W.J. Mueller. The carved frieze over the pediment is by prolific local carver and freemason E H Bailey, silversmith to Queen Victoria. He carved the statue of Nelson in Trafalgar Square, and several of his pieces are in the city's art gallery.

Continue up Park Street to turn left into Great George Street.

The corner house has a plaque noting that this was home to Henry Cruger, the only man to serve as an elected representative in both England and North America. He was a member of the 'Flying Squad' a bunch of young tearaways who refused to spend all evening in the same place and so pioneered pub crawls. There is often some confusion, especially in American records, between him and his father, who had the same name and was also in Bristol for a time. As a politician, Cruger often claimed the support of common people, such as sailors, but was accused of inciting riotous behaviour during elections. From 1808 this building was Chilcott's jewellers and silversmiths. The side entrance was for the pawnbroking business, to allow embarrassed clients some privacy.

Proceed up Great George Street to the monumental staircase of St George's on the right.

The site was an overflow graveyard to the ancient parish church of St Augustine-the-Less, now The Royal Hotel on College Green. Despite the church itself being on a street with large mansions, St George's parish included the dock area of Hotwells, so it had a large population of poor in need of charity. The church was the only one in the city completely paid for by a building fund established after the Napoleonic Wars rather than by local benefactors. It is now a popular music venue with cafe. It recently featured in an episode of Channel 4's 'Bone Detectives'. While preparing the ground for the building's extension, archaeologists discovered bones from several bodies which showed knife marks. It seems they were used to train surgeons, possibly from Bristol Royal Infirmary. One of the surgeons was Richard Smith who lived nearby and had been charged with bodysnatching. The graves were placed on the site with the poorest downhill. As in life, so in death.

Uphill on Great George Street is the Royal Colonnade, built about 1820 and the first neo-classical terrace in the city. Opposite is the Georgian House museum built by William Paty for the Pinney family of West India merchants. Pero's Bridge on the waterfront is named after one of their slave/servants. They are often described as unscrupulous slave owners, but the story is a far more complicated and interesting one. An ancestor, the Nonconformist minister Azariah Pinney, escaped execution and was sent to Nevis after his involvement in the Monmouth uprising. His descendants befriended the poets Coleridge and Southey; Wordsworth stayed in their house in Devon. Charles Pinney even proposed to the daughter of abolitionist Wilberforce. He was refused, not for being a slave owner, but for being absentee and for lending money to others, so he had no way of preventing abuse in the colony. He was the inexperienced young mayor at the time of the 1831 riots.

Continue up the hill to the corner of Brandon Hill Park.

Its name is allegedly from a chapel or hermitage dedicated to St Brendan. In 1565 the town's attorney built a windmill on its former site. When George III recovered his health, the city demonstrated its joy on March 5 1789 by firing canons all day from the top of the hill, and the city was illuminated with candles in windows that night. Industrial quantities of alcohol were also consumed, of course.

The near corner is clear of walling. This was the site of Bethesda Chapel, purchased for George Mueller (no relation of to the artists of this name) who founded the huge orphanage at Ashley Down in the 19th century. He often claimed to have prayed for funds and they were forthcoming. But he had a major patron, the fellow German and member of the Plymouth Brethren, C.W. Finzel. Finzel's sugar refinery survives near the former Georges Brewery south of Bristol Bridge. He is said to have donated £1,000 per year to the orphanage. He was also involved in the port improvements.

Spend some time exploring the park and take in the fine views to the south and west. If the tower is open, it provides even better views.

From George Street head up to Charlotte Street and follow the park to take the next entrance towards Berkeley Square.

This was built by the near-ubiquitous Paty family. It was planned in 1787, but due to economic problems was not completed till c.1800. This private park was laid out from the 1780s. In the downhill corner nearest Park Street is the top tier of John Norton's 1851 high cross, which is all that remains. It was vandalised and then rescued from the 1950 College Green levelling and moved here in 1956. Continue down Berkeley Avenue to the top of Park Street.

Opposite are 3 of the city's most important Victorian buildings, which represent her claim to civic culture.

To the left, on the corner of University Road, is the Venetian Gothic style Philosophical Institution. It moved here when the organisation outgrew its site further down the hill.

It was designed by the prolific local architects Foster and Ponton in 1872 and resembles Foster & Wood's facade for Colston Hall. It housed a library, museum and lecture halls. It was home to the Philosophical Society which promoted science and the arts. Also resident there were the Library Society and many scientific and cultural groups. Pevsner described it as "the West Country's greatest compliment to Ruskin". The facade was embellished with the civic coat of arms and those of leading citizens. The capitals show the heads of various animals and some plants that were displayed in the museum.

But by 1893 the institution was heavily in debt, so a wealthy benefactor bailed it out on condition the council took over the building to ensure public access. It was bombed in the war and the facade's details were lost. In 1940 the surviving contents were moved next door to the art gallery, while the building became the university refectory and is now a restaurant.

Adjoining this to the right is the art gallery purpose-built by Sir W. H. Wills. The architect was his cousin Frank Wills. It is on the site of the old Rifle Drill Hall, a popular venue for exhibitions, entertainments and charity fairs. The grandiose facade is a mixture of classical and baroque. It shows symbols of architecture, painting and sculpture, in true merchant prince style. It is probably the only building in the city built with no regard to cost.

The biggest and most impressive of the trio is the Wills Memorial Building. It is part of Bristol University, and claimed to be the last Gothic building constructed in England. It commemorates tobacco magnate and benefactor H.O. Wills. It was built between 1915 and

1925, by George Oatley in the Perpendicular Gothic style, echoing the style of many local parish churches. It is home to Great George, a 9 ton bell.

Take time to gaze up at the building's fantastic array of gargoyle-like masks portraying university staff. Spend some time in the museum and art gallery if you wish. From the restaurant, turn right from Park Street into University Road.

On the left is the Eastern Orthodox Church of the Nativity of the Mother of God. It was built by the Irvingite Apostolic Church in 1888 after relocating from St Mary-on-the-Quay.

In the next block on the left is Bristol Grammar School, founded in 1532 to educate the city's poor boys. The present buildings date from the mid-19th century when it had become a major public school. All classes were held in its massive hall. These buildings were designed by Foster and Wood in the 1870s and the interior may be viewed on Doors Open Day in September.

Continue straight ahead to the next junction to enter Tyndall's Park through the ornate gates. Veer up to the left towards the Royal Fort mansion and the end of this walk.

This is described by Pevsner as Bristol's finest Georgian villa. It was built from 1758 to 1761 by James Bridges for the Tyndalls family of bankers. His wooden model survives inside. It was on the site of the massive Civil War defences built by the Royalists under Prince Rupert. The 3-storeyed house has 3 different facades, often claimed to have been designed by 3 different architects. But it echoes the work of Capability Brown. The house was a feature in the landscape, and the landscape was part of the house design. It has superb rococo interiors, especially the plasterwork in the entrance and stairway. They are by Thomas Stocking who often worked with the various Patys. Thomas Paty did the stone carvings. Humphrey Repton designed the original gardens.

Until the Mayor's Mansion House was built on Queen Square, the mayor or other wealthy citizens provided accommodation for visiting dignitaries, such as Admiral Rodney in 1782. He was en route to London after the Battle of the Saints, the last battle fought against the

French in the Caribbean which established Britain's naval supremacy. John Weeks, publican of The Bush Inn on Corn Street, led a rushlight procession to greet the admiral. It was the first time Bristol had such a major celebration with no recorded fights or fatalities. The house is often open on Doors Open Day.

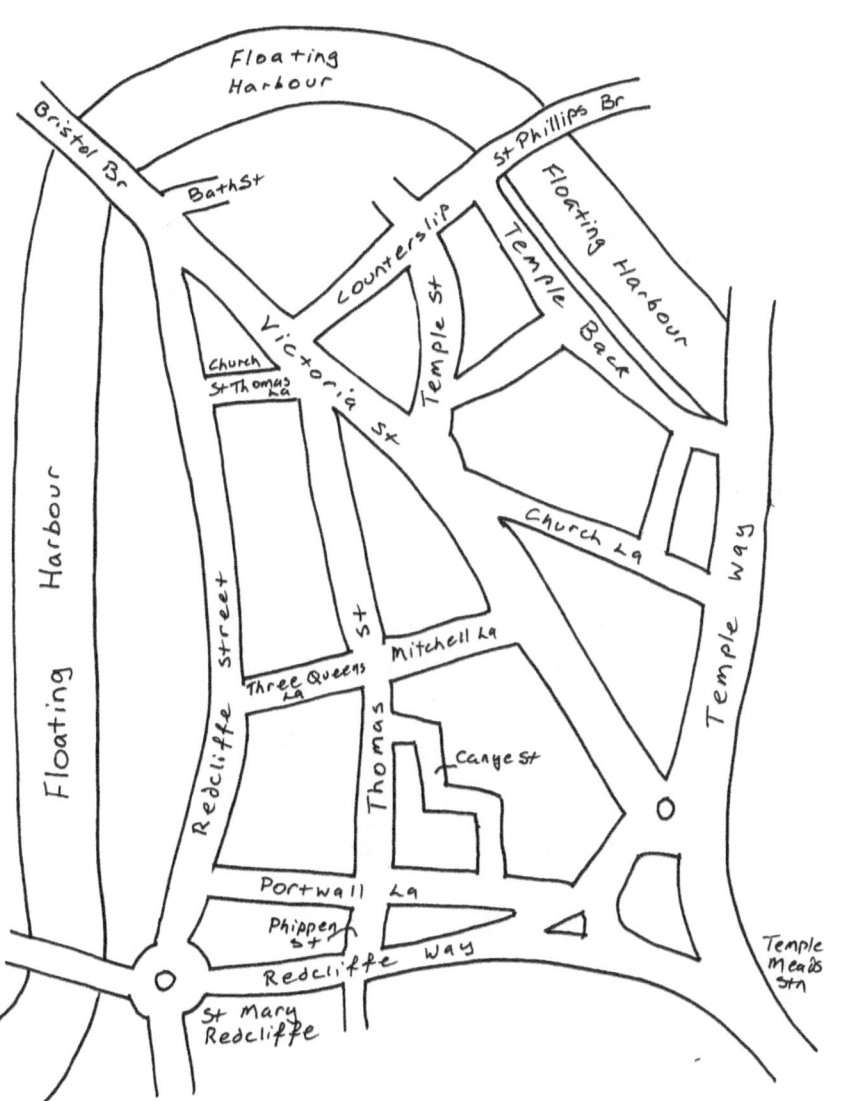

EIGHT

Long Way to Mary

Start: Bristol Bridge/WelshBack
End: St Mary Redcliffe
Length: Approx 1.5km/1 mile
Route: Partly on pedestrian walk ways, mostly quiet back streets. No slopes.
Public Transport: Any buses to city centre. Return by walking back along Redcliffe Parade/Queen Square to centre or catch one of many buses on Redcliffe Hill opposite the church.
PREAMBLE

To the north of Bristol Bridge was the ancient church of St Nicholas. It was built into the old town wall and partly rebuilt in 1503. It was spacious, with one of the city's finest altars which was reached by twelve steps and a black and white marble pavement over a busy but narrow gate. St Nicholas gate had a clock and a statue of Henry II who was educated in the parish. But by the 18th century the gate was becoming increasingly dangerous due to its narrowness and risks of collapse. Both John Wood of Bath and the crane builder/engineer John Padmore were consulted for repairs. John Wesley barely survived a fall from his horse there. The basement, with its entrance to the river, supported almost the whole length of the church and as a vault for burials it included a chapel for the guild of the Holy Cross. Its tower was an impressive timber structure encased in lead. The commissioners for the rebuilding of Bristol Bridge offered the vestry £1,400 for the damages of damage to the church and £1,000 more for building a replacement. They rebuilt without disturbing the human remains. The tower was then found to be unstable, so was also replaced. The engineers were James Bridges who fled the city and was completed by Thomas Paty.

The church was gutted during World War II and lost its rococo interior; the roofless structure was threatened with demolition. But it has been restored, and after decades as a local museum, the local tourist office, and home to regional archaeology services, it is now a church without a parish.

Henry II's charter of 1164 gave citizens of Redcliffe the same privileges as those of Bristol. But the freemen of Bristol had many, sometimes violent, disputes with the Berkeley family, Lords of Bedminster Manor. The disputes were largely resolved when the new stone bridge united the two regions. Bristol became a county as well as a town in 1373.

Donations to its chapel helped fund its other bridges. Until the 20th century it remained the city's only bridge crossing the Avon, at its lowest fordable point. When the first bridge was built, some sources claim the two regions were equal in wealth. But the north had the larger port, and many wealthy merchants. The southern parishes rose in wealth, and their Stallage Cross became the site of a huge market.

The parish of Redcliffe was part of the manor of Bedminster in Somerset, so was separate from Bristol. In 1145 land adjoining the river was given to the Knights Templar who built an oval church c.1150 and formed the region called Temple Fee. Around the time of the order's suppression in 1312 the church was rebuilt in its present rectangular shape. Barratt claimed the lean was caused by the force of the swinging bells, a belief still held by some locals. But a third stage was added in c.1460, in an attempt to correct it. By 1772 the top of the tower was three foot nine inches from perpendicular.

It was fully parochial by 1339, serving the local population. Its north east corner had a weavers' chapel, dedicated to their patron, St Katherine. It was the finest in the region. Its screen survives in St Stephen's church. The city purchased this church from Henry VIII with its lands at Temple Meads..The church was beautified in 1701 which cost three hundred pounds, of which Edward Colston contributed a third.

But the decline of the huge wool industry in the late 17th century turned this into the city's poorest area. In 1722 there were one hundred and nineteen clothiers south of the Avon; by 1784 there were only 22, though there were 4 or 5 new cotton mills. Edward Colston was born there and left legacies to fund several schools. Less known was Samuel Gist who was probably the son of a weaver and was born here. He was and educated at Queen Elizabeth Hospital, and sent to Virginia as a shop boy. On his death he left huge legacies in England and the USA. But this book is not about plugging other books by this author.

The church of St Thomas the Martyr was a chapel of ease to St Mary Redcliffe, built to save parishioners travelling to the mother church. It was founded in 1210 and later enlarged and rebuilt as a fine 15th century church. It was in the Perpendicular Gothic style, the scaled-down form that followed the Black Death and consequent loss of skilled tradesmen. As this and Temple were the only parish churches south of the river, they were significantly larger than those to the north. The parish was home to many clothiers and established several well-funded charities. In 1292 Simon Burton founded the parish almshouse and is buried there, so was a chantry where the beneficiaries prayed for him. In the 17th century several charities were founded on Temple Street. Dr Thomas White left £40 in his will per year for Temple Hospital, for 9 men and 3 women, and Thomas Stephens house for 12 women. White became a popular preacher and rector of St Dunstans in the West, London. He held several valuable posts at St Paul's, and St Georges Windsor which provided funds for his many charities. In 1711 Colston founded a school to educate local children and teach the established church catechism. Just inside Temple gate were two hospital/almshouses. The Weavers' Hall on Temple Street was for poor women, supported with 1 shilling per week from the company.

Before the mother church of St Mary was completed, it was the burial place of several Canynge family members, and Sir William Penn was baptised there. The parish became so poor, it could not afford to maintain its extension of the Redcliffe water pipe or its almshouse. Queen Elizabeth I gave permission to hold a market, an early job-creation scheme to bring trade, and therefore money, into the area. Latimer records how In 1828 the market held in Thomas Street was suppressed. A new wool hall i.e. the present one, was built for £4,400 from the compensation they received from the Corporation. But it was not a financial success and closed in 1834. The market was replaced with a cattle market at Temple Meads which cost £17,400. One of the first sales at the new market was the wife of a man called Gardner of Felton who "knocked her down" for £5 10s. This author will not use this opportunity to mention that this incident is included in her book on wife selling.

St Thomas' church has a very good reredos of 1716, the only survivor in the region. It also has a rare early Royal Arms from 1637. The body of the church was rebuilt by local man James Allen from 1781 to 1793 and major alterations were made between 1878 and 1890 by W V Gough.

But after World War II, the area lost most of its housing, and so its population. When the last vicar retired in 1940 there was no replacement. The last service was in 1982. It is now in the care of the Redundant Churches Fund and it can be hired for events.

Redcliffe Street was the main road from Bristol to the south, and home to many large merchants' houses. The most famous of these belonged to the merchant prince William Canynge. He has 2 tombs in St Mary Redcliffe, as a merchant and, following his wife's death, as a monk after he retired to Westbury-on-Trym to the north of the city. Nearby on the floor is an unusual memorial to his cook, showing the tools of his trade, and on the wall a plaque to a niece of the actor David Garrick, all in the south crossing of the church. A finely carved fireplace survives from Canynge's house in the former Savages' 'wigwam' now renamed 'Bristol 1904 Arts in the garden of the Red Lodge. A 15th century tiled floor is in the British Museum.

To enable the piers of first stone Bristol Bridge to be built, a channel was dug to divert the river. It ran from Temple Harratz (now Temple Meads station) to Redcliffe Hill. The town walls were built within this boundary. During the Civil War this combination became an impregnable stretch of the city's defences, and is now the route of Redcliffe Way.

The harbour was enlarged between 1239 and 1247 by rerouting the Frome into St Augustine's Reach. It had a muddy base, which minimised damage to ships at low tide. This expansion led to competition for funds between the parishes of St Stephens and St Nicholas'. It may have been the reason for the founding of St Stephen's.

In the 18th century the regions of Temple, St Stephens and Redcliffe were dominated by industries such as glass and sugar houses, brewing, distilling and pottery, all of which created huge levels of air pollution.

St Mary Redcliffe was described by Pevsner as the parish church that most wanted to be a Cathedral, and many visitors arriving at Temple Meads assume it to be so. Leland claimed "it goes beyond all parish churches in England I have ever seen". Its origins are obscure and its spire was damaged in a storm in 1445 and not repaired until the nineteenth century, reflecting the regions's economic history. The main entrance was on Redcliffe Hill, and was to the west, as is traditional, so worshippers move towards the light in the east. The north porch is unusual as it is on 2 levels, and shows strong Islamic and Gothic elements which are often attributed to the city's trading links with Portugal. It faced the homes of most of its parishioners and was the closest door to the port. Inside, stairs lead to a chamber above where the prodigy Thomas Chatterton discovered old documents which allowed him to pretend were the works of the medieval Rowley or Rowlie. This became a tourist attraction in the wake of his death, for visitors including Dr Johnstone. Above the south porch which leads into the churchyard was a wainscotted room where the vestry met. The medieval church had many altars to saints such as Stephen, Blaze, and Nicholas. On a high wall near the west entrance is the armour and memorial to Admiral William Penn who was born in Bristol in 1621. He was captain at 21 and led England to victory as General in the first Dutch War at the age of 32.

This walk meanders south from the old city to see some little-known parts of the southern districts.

THE AMBLE

Start at the southern end of Bristol Bridge.

On the corner of Victoria Street is No. 1 Redcliffe Street, former site of the E.S. & A. Robinson building. In 1963 it became the city's first true tower block. But it was so controversial that the university's architectural students burnt effigies in protest against it.

Across Victoria Street on the corner of Bath Street, is a fine Byzantine former pub from the 1870s, the Talbot Inn. Its predecessor was the local headquarters of Henry 'Orator' Hunt. He campaigned to become a local MP before his involvement in the 1819 Peterloo massacre in Manchester. In 1807 he had opened a brewery at Jacob's Wells, and attempted to stand as a local MP but was refused permission as he was not a freeholder or free burgess. Hunt's followers were accused of smashing the windows of the Council House and White Lion Hotel, and of pelting the new MP, Mr Bathurst, with mud and sticks. Hunt calmed the mob by offering them free beer but more attacks followed.

Bath Street was built by the Paty family as part of the redevelopment leading to — and helping to pay off the debts of — Bristol Bridge. It was to provide access to the main Bath Road. Until then, the route had meandered through narrow, rundown streets. This allowed locals to empty chamber pots onto travellers. The rank of houses on the south side are original; the rest were devoured by the Courage Brewery.

Turn right into Redcliffe Street to the first break in the buildings to see a large ceramic sculpture.

This is 'Exploration', by Phillipa Threlfal of 1991.

Cross Redcliffe Street into Thomas Lane.

On the left is the redundant church of St Thomas the Martyr, the last of the city churches to be rebuilt (except the tower) by James Allen in 1793. Allen was a talented local architect, but was apparently marginalised by the force that was the Paty family. He designed several impressive country houses, but they have all been demolished. He deserved to be more than a mere footnote in his city's architectural history.

Across the lane from the church is the Seven Stars pub. A plaque commemorates its role in the abolition of the slave Trade. Thomas Clarkson gathered information from sailors here. His access to the Merchant Venturers' shipping records showed the mortality of sailors on slave ships to be 5 times higher than normal. This was a major reason for the mens' dislike of the trade. Only the most desperate sailed on slave ships. This probably contributed to the high levels of mortality and of brutality towards slaves.

Next to this, on the corner of St Thomas Street, is the Fleece venue. It was built by R.S. Pope in 1830 for St Thomas' Parish as a warehouse and market hall but is now a music venue. It replaced the wool hall, the only place where wholesale wool could be sold. This ensured high standards and accurate weights to prevent fraud.

Turn left into St Thomas Street East.

Note a rank of 4 shops to the left, dated 1456. But they are too tidy, without the overhanging storeys characteristic of the time, so are more likely to be 17th century.

Turn right into Victoria Street. This was laid out in 1865, a mere 25 years after it was first proposed, to give access to the city from Temple Meads station.

Cross over into Counterslip and continue to the river.

The name records a landing stage for boats going upstream to Bath. Rising above this is the listed Shot Tower of 1967. It replaced William Watts' original on Redcliffe Hill which was demolished for post-war road widening. Today it would be listed.

Turn right into Temple Back.

Running along the riverside is a large ornate Byzantine-style building. It was the electricity generating station, built by the council in 1890. It housed 18 coal-fired steam engines and had a pair of 180 foot high chimneys. It has been developed, with only a facade from the old building left.

Turn right into Water Lane, then left into Temple Street to reach the gateway to the ancient church of Temple or Holy Cross.

This was built c.1390. When its tilting was noticed, attempts were made to correct it while building the second stage c.1460. But it was never finished, possibly as it was too dangerous. It is now 5 feet out of vertical. It was gutted in the Blitz and is now cared for by English Heritage. During World War II sappers tried to pull it down for being unsafe. It was said to have been built on wool sacks, but this is a metaphor for the wealth that paid for it. The region was low-lying, marshy and prone to floods. Like many others in the city, the adjoining graveyard became overcrowded. It was closed under the 1854 Health in Towns Act. It was then landscaped to provide welcome open space for recreation. The building has now been restored as a welcome open space.

Return to Victoria Street.

Note several old shops and pubs including The Shakespeare, of 1636. Cross Victoria Street and turn next right into Mitchell Lane, then left into St Thomas Street. Follow this towards the busy Redcliffe Way. Before its end it becomes Phippin Street.

Portwall Lane follows the inside of the 13th century town wall. With its ditch on the far side, this was the most secure defence in the

Civil War. Tolls were collected on goods entering and exiting the city to pay for the wall's maintenance. Temple Gate on St Thomas Street was widened and rebuilt in 1734 to deal with the increasing traffic, but was demolished in 1808. Redcliffe Gate on Redcliffe Way was rebuilt in 1731 and demolished in 1771.

On the left facing the busy Redcliffe Way is the last of many houses that obscured the approach to St Mary Redcliffe until they were cleared away in 1842. A plaque notes it was built in 1749 for the use of the schoolmaster of St Thomas' parish whose son, the poet Thomas Chatterton was born here in 1752. It is now a cafe. Attached to it is the facade of the schoolhouse which is dated 1779 but its style was by then old fashioned. The rest of it was demolished in 1939 for widening of Redcliffe Way. This makes it a very early example of the modern plague of facadism. A column commemorating Thomas stood in the churchyard across the road. It was on the north side as he had committed suicide, or self-murder, though recent research challenges this. He was proclaimed a prodigy for his poems about historical events, but was then exposed as a fraud.

He is now more famous for his suicide which it was feared would inspire others. He also wrote poems inspired by the surrounding countryside, especially Avon Gorge. This makes him a forerunner of Romantic poets such as Coleridge and Southey. Some claim his work was better than Gray and Mason. In the late 18th century the muniment, or records, room in St Mary Redcliffe church became a tourist attraction for visitors, including Johnson and Boswell.

Across Redcliffe Way is St Mary Redcliffe church, with its wealth of history and a fine cafe in the undercroft. If the church is open, it is well worth a visit. Pevsner described it as the parish church that most wished to be a cathedral, and many people assume it to be so.

CHAPTER EIGHT

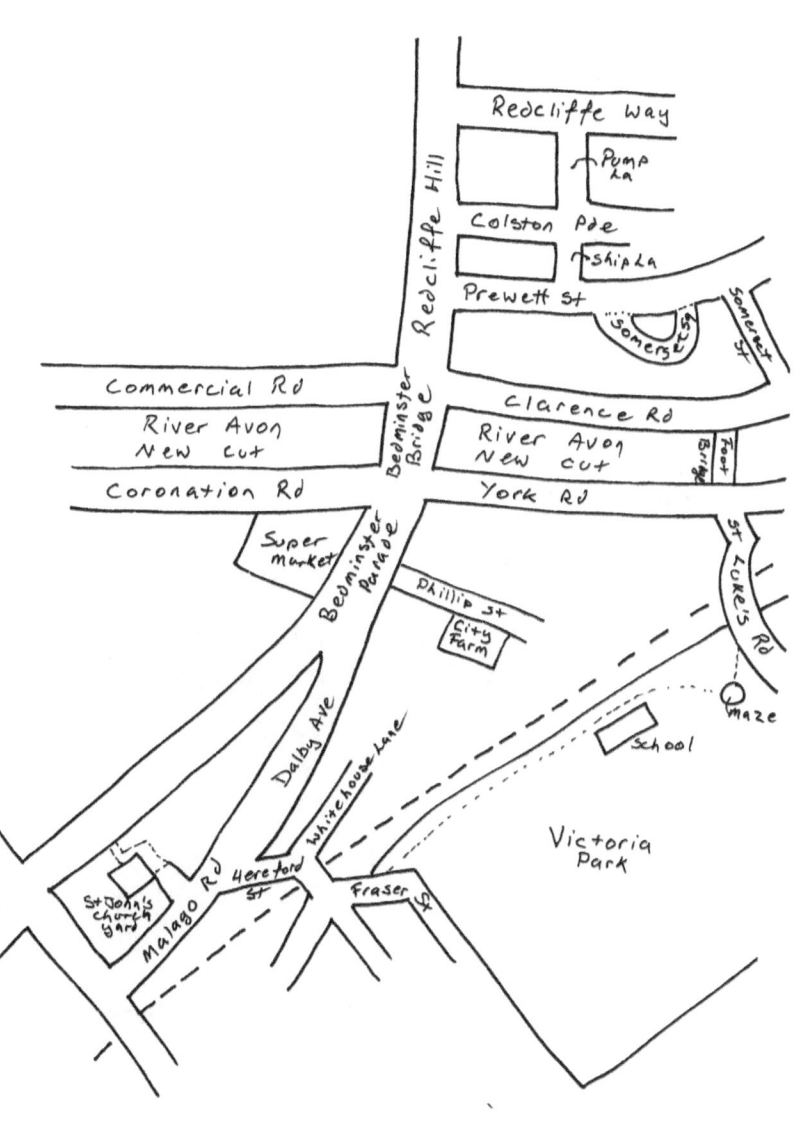

NINE

Mary's Mother John

Start: St Mary Redcliffe church
End: St John's churchyard, off East Street shopping precinct, Bedminster
Length: Approx. 2km/1 mile
Route: Mixture of quiet back streets, a public park and crossing five busy roads. A few gentle slopes, no steps
Public Transport: Walk from city centre or Temple Meads station to start. Return along East Street by bus or on foot
PREAMBLE
This walk follows on from Walk no. 7 so they can be done in sequence. It goes from daughter to mother church. It also traces part

of the Norman water pipe, the only source of fresh water for the parish. Before being damaged by wartime bombs, it ran from springs about two miles away at Knowle to outlets on Redcliffe Hill and at St Thomas's church. Every year parishioners walk the pipe's route, the revival of a practice which may date back to c.1190, making it the oldest such event. This walk also passes through Victoria Park, where a water maze is based on a roof boss in St Mary Redcliffe.

St Mary Redcliffe was the daughter church of the much older but now largely forgotten rural church of St John's, Bedminster. Other daughters were at Knowle and Abbots Leigh. The church of St Thomas to the north on the same road was in its turn a chapel of ease to St Mary Redcliffe.

The church of St Mary Redcliffe dominates the skyline of Bristol, and is one of the finest parish churches in the country. Leland claimed "It goes beyond all parish churches in England I have ever seen", so it is worth spending some time exploring before embarking on the walk. It had many altars, including to saints Stephen, Blaze and Catherine.

Early records of it are scant and it is first mentioned c.1160. In 1445 a great tempest 'threw down' the tower and caused extensive damage to the roof which allowed the rain to ruin much of its interior. Its 14th century two-level north porch shows elements of gothic and islamic styles, so probably based on Portugese designs as this was Bristol's major trading partner at the time, for sherry and cork to seal the bottles of it. Above it was the room where Chatterton found the ancient documents which inspired his historical forgeries. It later became a tourist attraction.

The main entrance was to the west, facing Redcliffe Hill. When people entered, they were walking towards the rising sun. In the 18th century, a room over the south porch was wainscotted and used for vestry meetings. The Lady Chapel housed the grammar school; a carved statue of Queen Elizabeth I survives from it in the mariners' chapel to the right inside the main door. Below this is allegedly a narwahl tusk, but it is from an elephant.

In the centre of the churchyard was an elegant cross described by

William of Worcester where sermons were preached. Local antiquarian Dr Barratt claims the yard held many notable tombs and crypts. But 1755 the church and grounds were extensively and expensively improved. William Hogarth was commissioned to paint a trio of paintings for the new altar. They are now displayed together and referred to as a triptych. This was his only piece for an Anglican church. Claims have been made that much of the work was by local artists, whom he praised, but invoices show his involvement. The frame was by Thomas Paty. But at a huge 16 metres by 8 1/2, it was too large and fell out of favour when the church was again reorganised. After a failed attempt at a sale in the 19th century, it moved to St Nicholas' church in the city centre. St Nicholas has been a local history museum, the tourist office, and the local archeology office, and is now a church again. Only in Bristol would such an important work be so shoddily treated.

There is some fine gilded ironwork by William Edney, rescued from the bombed Temple church. Look for the tiny mouse in it. Monuments include 2 effigies to the merchant prince William Canynge, with his wife and as a cleric at Westbury. A large slab on the floor nearby is dedicated to his cook, showing the tools of his trade. There is a monument to Arabella Bridges Schaw, a niece of David Garrick. High on the wall of the nave is a memorial with armour. This commemorates Admiral Sir William Penn, diplomat, general and father of the founder of Pennsylvania.

Redcliffe Hill was the main route from Bristol into Somerset, lined with pubs and shops from early times. But the west side was bombed in World War II. The road widening destroyed buildings including William Watts' shot tower and the resulting rubble was used to raise the roadway to its present level.

THE AMBLE

Start at St Mary Redcliffe church which is of course worth a visit.

It is a fascinating church to explore, but for this walk, the maze roof boss is particularly worthy of note. After entering the church from the main, north entrance, turn left down the aisle. Just before the crossing, look up at the roof to see a gold boss in the shape of a maze. This provided the inspiration for the water maze later in this walk. Take time to explore the church then exit via the south door into the main churchyard. A chapel in the centre of the churchyard became an Elizabethan grammar school which later moved into the Lady chapel. The ruin was removed, together with the ancient cross, when the churchyard was tidied up in 1763. The omnipresent Paty family were again involved. A local paper claimed the churchwarden was carting away soil for his brickworks. This horrified locals, but no action was taken. This clean-up is why the churchyard was far less crowded than those of the old city. When the latter's graveyards closed on health grounds in 1854, this one continued to accept burials.

But when Brunel's Port Railway needed to pass beneath it, the graves were moved to a new site opposite Arnos Vale Cemetery for which the parish received £2,500 in compensation. It seems the tunnel running beneath here was made by 'cut and cover' rather than the usual, more dangerous and expensive method of tunnelling.

On the embankment to the left is a tombstone to the church cat, a tabby called Puss which appeared in 1912 and decided to stay. Adopted by the verger, it sat on his lap while he played the church organ. It was cared for by the ladies in Fry's House of Mercy nearby. The cat burial shows the churchyard was no longer consecrated. To its left is a large tombstone to Thomas Chatterton's father.

In the far left corner a large lump of metal sticks out of the ground. It is part of a tramline blown up on Redcliffe Hill which landed here during the Blitz.

From the south entrance of the church, follow the path parallel with Redcliffe Hill to the corner of Colston Parade. Turn right onto the main road to see the outlet of the 12th century lion-headed water pipe. It is partly obscured by the raised road level.

Samuel Plimsoll MP was born at nine Colston Parade. Known as the 'Sailors' Friend', he campaigned for marine safety. Scores of young men were sent to sea in overloaded, 'coffin' ships which often sank. This allowed the owners to claim the insurance. He invented the Plimsoll line which marks the level to which a ship can be safely loaded in the water. A bust of him was erected on Hotwell Road, but moved in 2005 to the floating harbour and in 2010 placed at Capricorn Quay. For now.

Turn left along Colston Parade, the finest street in the parish.

When this street was built, it was prime real estate. The gates at each end were locked and the sexton had the key, making it a precursor of the modern gated community.

About half way along is Fry's House of Mercy which provided accommodation for poor women of the parish. It was built in 1784 by a local pin maker to commemorate the early death of his son. It was gutted in the Blitz but has been restored.

Two buildings at the end were built by Thomas Paty in 1755. The end house had a great room for parish meetings, with fine plasterwork and Colston's coat of arms. It was home to the sexton, who had to cater for such meetings. Both buildings were damaged in the Blitz and are now flats. Beyond them is The Ship Inn, a fine eighteenth century pub.

Turn right down Ship Lane to Somerset Square.

This was built in 1756 when much of the city was being redeveloped. It was an elite development, open to the south, with fresh air and grand views of Dundry. It had fine Georgian town houses, including one owned by the Duke of Beaufort. In the centre is a Grade II listed structure, carved in sandstone. It is claimed to be a former conduit head, but there is no sign of the conduit, though it may be on the line of the Redcliffe Pipe. It is also claimed to have been made of demolished church buildings, but this would date it to the 18th century, and it shows none of the erosion that would be expected. It could be an architectural folly used as a garden ornament, possibly even from after the last war.

Turn left along Prewett Street.

Further along on the right is The Bell Inn. At the time of writing it was long abandoned.

Look into the rear of the large hotel on the left to see a round brick building. This is the region's last surviving glass cone, dating from about 1780, a remnant of one of the most extensive and smoke-producing industries, manufacturing Bristol's famous blue glass. Hotwells spa water was exported in glass bottles. Redcliffe Caves provided the glass, which makes them quarries.

From 1812 it was part of the artificial fertiliser company run by Alderman Thomas Proctor, the first man to import guano into this country. He tested his fertiliser on the local churchyard grass. He also planted trees along the New Cut to encourage locals to promenade on Sundays for their health. Proctor donated the Mayor's Mansion on Clifton Down to the city and built the nearby Gothic drinking fountain to commemorate the granting of the Downs to the public as an open space in perpetuity. He was a generous donor to the 19th century rebuilding of St Mary Redcliffe, both as a churchwarden and anonymously as 'Nil Desperandum'.

The next stretch of the walk is less pleasant due to busy roads, but you soon reach Victoria Park.

Turn right down Somerset Street, cross Clarence Road at the lights and take the 'banana bridge' across the river. Cross York Road into St Luke's Road, and follow its right-hand side under the railway bridge to the first entrance to Victoria Park. Veer left to the water maze.

The story of the maze and the water pipe can be read on bricks round the sides. It was built in 1984 by Bristol Water to divert the sewage which was discharged into the floating harbour. It also diverted the storm water to prevent a repeat of the disastrous floods of 1968 which damaged about 3,000 homes and killed 8 people.

Victoria Park was purchased from the Greville Smyth family of Ashton Court for £20,678 in 1888. A further £8,656 was spent landscaping it before its opening in 1891. It aimed to promote healthy recreation and was later called the 'Durdham Down of the South'. The area had many unhealthy industries whose workers crowded into the cramped, unsanitary terraces.

Marching across the lower reaches of the park are small tombstone-like markers showing the Redcliffe Pipe's route. Maps from the 1870s show the park surrounded by terraced housing. The houses along St Lukes Road were demolished to make the park.

Most of the land was owned by Greville Smyth of Ashton Court who also donated the land for Bedminster Park at Ashton. As soon as this park was built, the surrounding streets filled with middle class housing, as the park made this a desirable location.

Near the corner of Hill Street and St Luke's Avenue was an open-air swimming pool. It was built to ensure dockworkers and sailors learnt how to swim, so they would not be drowned at work. It became redundant in the 1970s when the docks closed, not because locals had become soft and preferred indoor swimming.

During World War II, the park was dug up for allotments. Apparently they were never damaged or robbed. Some cite this as proof of the honesty of locals, but soldiers were camped in the park.

Round the far side was a bandstand which was an open-air school for children too frail for normal education. Many had tuberculosis and/or rickets and would normally have been denied education. But they had nature lessons and small classes and were often envied by pupils at other schools. They were so dedicated, they waded through snow to get to school only to find that the ink had frozen in their ink pots.

At the highest point near the lodge was an ornate fountain topped by an eagle, with lion's head spouts. Downhill was a cannon from HMS Daedalus, aimed at Clifton, or at Wills' tobacco factory. Along with the iron fencing and gates, these artefacts were removed during World War II to make munitions. However, they were probably the wrong sort of metal and so never used.

A path leads from the maze straight up the hill to a grove of maple trees on the left. They were planted to mark the 500th anniversary of Cabot's 'discovery' of North America, and a stone commemorates this.

You can take time to explore the park, and follow the path down the far side to exit into Frazer Street.

Alternatively, follow the path curving round the hill to the right and along the railway line to leave the park and pass in front of St Mary Redcliffe schools. Re-enter the park and continue along the railway line.

Before the park was established, this was the site of a rope walk.

Turn right into Frazer Street. Pass Bedminster station then turn right through the railway tunnel. Take the pedestrian crossing over Whitehouse Lane. Pass the grass-roofed but at the time of writing abandoned headquarters of the city farms association. Cross Malago Road which follows the line of the flood-prone stream of the same name. Turn left and continue till you turn right into St John's Road. Several steps lead up to the former churchyard, or you can detour to enter it on the far side.

On the far side of the park is the footprint of the ornate Gothic church of 1855 by antiquarian John Norton. He was responsible for the latest version of the city's high cross, the church at Stoke Bishop and part of Tyntesfield. The building here replaced an ancient country church which may have dated back to the 10th century. But as with much of Bedminster, it was burnt by Prince Rupert in 1645, and rebuilt in 1663. On Easter and Whitsun, young people used to go there for a 'revel'. In November 1822, constables were sent to this churchyard at midnight when they found 6 people disinterring the remains of a young woman. A fight broke out involving rapiers and pistols and eventually 5 or 6 were arrested. The outcome is not known.

It had a huge and very active congregation, but was gutted in 1940. Though its restoration was repeatedly promised, it was eventually demolished in 1969. The gate opposite your entry leads to the once-flourishing East Street shopping precinct, now a shadow of itself thanks to years of government austerity.

You can catch a bus or walk back to the centre.

On the main road, just before ASDA you can take a detour. Turn right into Phillips Street for Windmill Hill City Farm.

This is a thriving community centre with organic gardens and animals, and of course, a cafe.

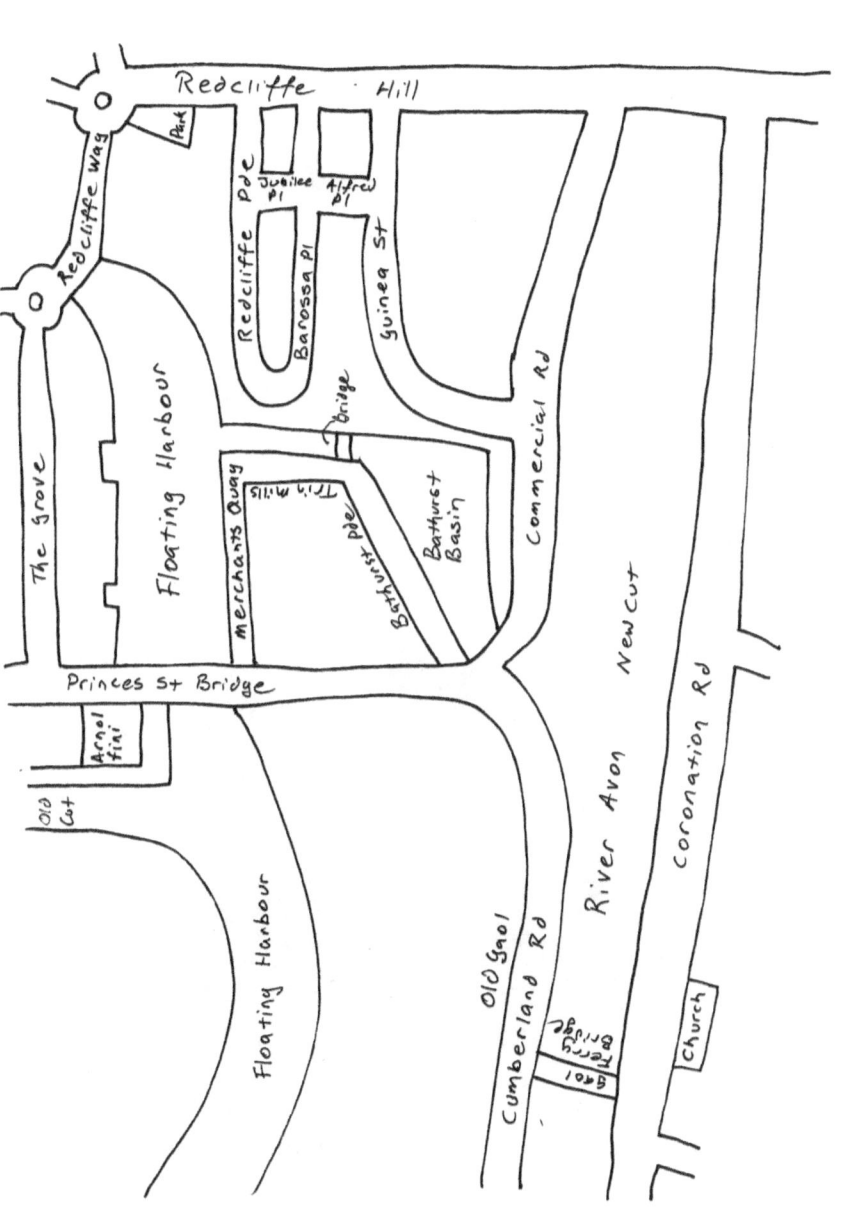

TEN

Passport to Bemmie

Start: The small park on corner of Redcliffe Hill & Redcliffe Way
End: Create Centre, Smeaton Road, Cumberland Basin
Length: 3km/1.5 miles
Route: Approximately half is on pedestrian paths, the rest follows busy roads. Almost the entire route is flat except for a long slope up and down. Steps up cliff face can be avoided by a ramp.

Public Transport: Walk from centre of town to start, or catch bus to Redcliffe Hill. Return via Harbour ferry from Pump House pub on the Floating Harbour or bus from Hotwells.

PREAMBLE

This walk explores Redcliffe Hill, then follows The Cut to the Cumberland Basin. Bristol and Bedminster have a long tradition of being proudly separate. Locals of a certain age joked of needing a passport to cross between them. The northern area was a major port which traded nationally and internationally. The southern parishes of St Thomas' and Temple had flourished from the various wool trades. But by the late 17th century this industry had declined. The south was also a major route southwards to the weirdness of Somerset. Those with keen ears could detect the locals' different accents, with more Germanic elements to the south.

Until the 20th century the only physical link between the two was Bristol Bridge, though there were several ferries. The south was slow to develop beyond the main port area. This allowed a wide range of Nonconformist groups to establish themselves, especially the many branches of Methodism that emerged after the death of Wesley, many of which were short-lived.

The River Avon is more than a physical feature. For centuries the economy to its north was bigger and more successful than that of the south. New post-war estates have struggled in the south, while gentrification has sent property prices in many northern suburbs soaring. The opulence of St Mary Redcliffe shows the huge wealth in the area in the past. This came from the mediaeval wool trade, then from the quays and shipbuilding as the main port expanded.

Brunel's Port Railway ran beneath Redcliffe Hill along the south side of the Floating Harbour and round the busy 19th century wharves.

Much of this walk follows the New Cut. It was a massive engineering project which began with the first sod turned near Mr Teast's shipyard at Wapping Wharf on 1 May 1804. It was completed in record time by a mixture of Irish and English navvies, the former doing the heaviest work. French prisoners of war were not involved;

this is yet another local myth. The mix of nationalities may have been out of necessity, or it may have exploited traditional animosity to urge each group to work harder than the other.

When The Cut was finished, a roast ox and plenty of beer were supplied for the workers. But the celebrations degenerated into a full-scale brawl which lasted for several days. The Irish retreated to their lodgings on Princes Street to collect their shillelaghs to continue the bloodshed. Constables were forced to call on the press gang, and the Riot Act was read. The bicentenary of this event was celebrated by locals with a ceilidh. No injuries were recorded, though music and dancing were involved. And small children.

The New Cut (as opposed to the Old Cut of the 13th century) runs from St Phillip's Marsh several miles upstream. It joins the Floating Harbour at the Cumberland Basin, which opened on 2 April 1809 when the first vessels entered Bathurst Basin. Brunel's SS Great Britain was built on the south side of the harbour, continuing a long tradition of local shipbuilding. But it was the final hurrah as high port charges were driving ships elsewhere, especially Liverpool. The long, winding river with the huge tidal surge had for centuries protected the port from storms and invasions. But it became a hindrance as ships grew larger and steam power became dominant. Even Wiltshire clothiers moved their trade from Bristol to Liverpool.

National changes also had an impact. The Industrial Revolution shifted the country's population and wealth to the Midlands and the North, so Bristol's trade along the River Severn declined. The Merchant Venturers had managed the docks, but were failing to deal with the problems at hand. Bristol Corporation took over full control of the docks under an act of 1848. In 1851 the Demerera ship hit some rocks, then the tide turned it to obstruct the river. After that, Bristol ceased to be a proper ocean port, though banana boats from the Caribbean continued for some time after World War II. Nor was it ever a port of departure for emigrants to North America, though some left for Canada from Bristol before World War 1.

THE AMBLE

Start at the small walled park opposite St Mary Redcliffe. This was the Quaker burial ground from 1665 until 1923. It was closed and given to the city in 1950. On the far side is a gate in the wall, the remains of a hermitage founded by Thomas, Lord Berkeley. The first hermit was John Sparkes from 1346. It houses tombstones to local families, ranging from infants to a 99 year old, from 1669. After World War II, children from the nearby school used to play football here. They recalled the graves being marked with numbered terracotta tiles, the details of which were held in the church. In the late 17th century Bristol Quakers suffered horrific persecution. Many were fined, imprisoned and even transported to the West Indies. Probably in response to this, many became successful businessmen, shipbuilders and industrialists.

This was the site of the Hospital of St John, an Augustinian house which was apparently founded by John Farcey or Farceyn. The first record of it is from a 13th century deed which allowed the house a supply of water from the Redcliff pipe. It seems to have housed sisters as well as brothers, which is rare. The chapel of the Holy Spirit in Redcliffe churchyard was made over to them but it was later given to the fraternity of the Holy Spirit so the community was in decline by 1387. By 1442 only 1 brother remained. The site was set back from the road until post-war widening demolished the intervening buildings. Behind the cell of the former hermitage are the Redcliffe Caves, a network of cellars dug out from the quayside. Others were dug from the houses on the clifftop as double and triple cellars. One of Bristol's many urban legends claims that the caves were used to store slaves. But this is nonsense. It is based on a guess by a local inhabitant when the cellars were unearthed during the building of the Port Railway. Redcliffe Pit itself seems to have been the result of digging for stone, possibly as ballast for outgoing boats.The red sand was used to make Bristol Blue Glass and in glazes by the many local potteries. It was also scattered on the floor to mop up spills in the many small pubs. Boys working there were part paid in alcoholic beverages, leading to the term, 'as happy as a sand boy'. Thus, they are not caves, but quarries.

Leave the park and turn left onto Redcliffe Way. Just before the bridge over the Floating Harbour, turn left along the waterside path, which was for many centuries a busy quay.

Set into the far cliff face are several gates, entrances to the caves. Lead waste was found here, a relic of William Watts' home on Redcliffe Hill where he produced the first lead shot. He poured molten lead through a colander from the top of his tower, to land in a barrel of water. The idea for this allegedly came to him in a dream, but more likely he noticed what happened when lead melted on roofs during fires.

Follow the path round to the right, past the outdoor activity centre on the waterside and the former fire station, now an occasional art gallery. Just before the quay turns left, steps on your left lead up the cliff face. Take these up to Redcliffe Parade.

The westernmost row of houses, i.e., furthest from St Mary, was built between 1768 and 1771 by local shipbuilder Sydenham Teast. They are impressive merchants' houses, with fine views of the harbour and access to fresh air. Beyond the end of this terrace is an older house with views the length of the harbour, the former Harbour Master's home. The eastern terrace was built by the King family of shipowners c.1800 to a plainer design. Turn right into Jubilee Place, then Alfred Place.

On the right-hand corner of Guinea Street is a small house, the former Armchair Inn, which had a half-size armchair above the door. This shows how small, and hence how numerous, local pubs were.

To the left directly in front is 10 Guinea Street, the largest of a trio of houses built in 1718 by slave trader Captain Saunders. They were in the already old-fashioned Dutch style which became popular with the arrival of William III's court. It has fine grotesques on keystones over the windows and featured in the David Olusogo tv series 'A House Through Time'.

Walk down Guinea Street past the Golden Guinea pub, with its links to the infamous African slave and other trades, then to the former Bristol General Hospital, now expensive private housing.

The hospital began as a few houses run by Quakers on the site of a former sugar factory. They were concerned at the number of injuries suffered by port workers and sailors. The only hospitals at the time were the Royal Infirmary or, for the very poor, St Peter's Hospital in what is now Castle Park. This shows another division within the city, that of of High Church Tories patronising the Infirmary while Low Church Anglicans and Dissenters were treated here. The main building, by W.B. Gyngell, dates from 1857 and included waterside cellars that were rented out to help fund the hospital.

To the right is the tunnel for Brunel's Port Railway which ran from Temple Meads round the docks. Further right is The Ostrich Inn, possibly dating from 1830 with parts from the 18th century or earlier. Rumours abound of slave tunnels running from it into the rock face which are of course nonsense.

Cross the footbridge.

The harbour railway and the old port area have been developed to form Merchants' Landing. Trin Mills, is named after the tidal double water mill which straddled the River Malago here. It was built by St Augustine's Abbey to generate income for St Catherine's Hospital to care for the local poor. It was also a leper hospital for women, the site of which became the huge Wills' tobacco factory, which is now a large supermarket.

Before the Floating Harbour was built this stretch of water was the outlet for the Malago Stream which flowed through Bedminster to the River Avon. The meaning of its name is unknown but its flow was infamously unreliable, and floods were common. When the New Cut was built between 1805 and 1809, the millpond was enlarged to form Bathurst Basin where ships moored while waiting to sail on the tide. It also hosted the mayor's annual duck shoot. During World War II, the entrance was sealed in case it was bombed and the harbour emptied. It has not been re-opened.

Veer to the left past a linked pair of Byzantine-style buildings on Bathurst Parade, which was named after Lord Bathurst MP.

These are former oil seed warehouses designed by W.B. Gyngell in 1874. Further along is a stone marking the old city boundary with Somerset which was here between 1373 and 1874. At the end of this row is the Louisiana pub, the former Bathurst Hotel, with its fine wrought iron railings from 1820. It has long been a popular music venue. A local myth claims there was a tunnel from here to the gaol.

The monumental wall are all that remains of the outer wall of the New Gaol built 1816–20 by H H Seward. It was rebuilt by R.S. Pope using cheaper materials after the 1831 riots.

After many decades of problems housing local criminals in filthy conditions, this modern well-ventilated prison was built. It was mostly for debtors from Newgate and for public executions which took place above the surviving listed gatehouse. These events were so popular and the area in front so narrow that spectators sometimes fell into the water. Most of the prison was destroyed with the city's other places of detention in the 1831 riots. It closed in 1883 when Horfield Prison replaced it and the site was sold to the Great Western Railway.

The city is awash with tales of slave holes and of manacles in basements, but many of these are from buildings which postdate abolition of the Atlantic slave trade. The most likely explanation is that citizens with secure cellars took in prisoners after the riots until more suitable accommodation was provided.

James Gardiner, former militia captain and Inspector of Bedminster Police, was governor for 40 years. He introduced major reforms such as photographing prisoners. With his wife, the matron, he raised funds and helped reform and re-settle them on their release. But by 1872, complaints were being made of the conditions there.

Across the New Cut is the church of St Paul by Charles Dyer. It was consecrated in 1831 by the local bishop who had voted against the Reform Act, so the event attracted considerable disturbances. This was a foretaste of the riots which erupted only 5 days later. They became the greatest public disturbance in 19th century Britain. The church was bombed in the Blitz and largely rebuilt in 1958. Its cellar contains a bomb shelter which is sometimes used for art exhibitions. The parish was long associated with sailors and dockworkers, and the clock on the tower is supported by a female figurehead.

Continue to the Gaol Ferry suspension bridge. It has been closed for repairs to the great inconvenience of locals. The council seems to be in no hurry to fix it.

This was built in 1935 to replace the ferry which had run since 1838, the approaches to which can still be seen by the waterside. On the opposite bank an archway leads to Acraman's Road. This allowed goods, especially bulky timber, to be transported from boats to a nearby timber yard.

Continue along the pavement until a path leads down to the waterside. At the time of writing, the chocolate path — named after its blocked surface — had been damaged by high tides, but the walk can be continued on the right hand side footpath.

Alternatively you can walk through the new harbourside developments. If it is in port, you can visit the reconstructed ship The Matthew, then follow the waters' edge to the left and visit Brunel's Great Western Steamship, before rejoining the walk at the Underfall Yard.

The Chocolate Path dates from c.1903 and was built on brick arches on earth which was removed to create the New Cut. It runs beside the long redundant Port Railway built by Brunel to transport goods for docks on the Floating Harbour. Unfortunately this has been collapsing for many years and the council sees it as a low priority.

At low tide this is a good place to watch birdlife, including herons which tend to congregate round the large drain outflows on the opposite bank. Otters have been sighted, and cormorants often fish here.

Pass a large pedestrian bridge.

This is the no-longer-swinging Vauxhall hydraulic bridge. It is named after the short-lived 18th century pleasure gardens to the right.

The path veers out to the left and narrows as it passes over the outlet for the Underfall Yard, where mud from the Floating Harbour is flushed out. The building of the Floating Harbour meant an end to several tidal mills on the River Avon, so this allowed their continuation. But by then the more reliable steam power was taking over to power mills, so it soon became redundant.

This is a popular place for black-headed gulls to play at low tide. Further along the water's edge are two former bonded tobacco warehouses built by Wills in the early 19th century.

Just past the first is a sign for the Sustrans cycle route, pointing to

Leigh Woods and the Pill cycle route. On the left is the former Ashton swing bridge. Before the huge Cumberland Basin swing bridge was built, this carried road traffic above, and rail traffic below. The furthest warehouse is now The Create Centre and Bristol Record Office where this author has spent far too much of her life.

A bus can take you back to the centre of town, or you can follow the same road towards the Floating Harbour to reach the Pump House pub and the ferry landing stage. If the steam train is running, it can take you back to the MShed museum.

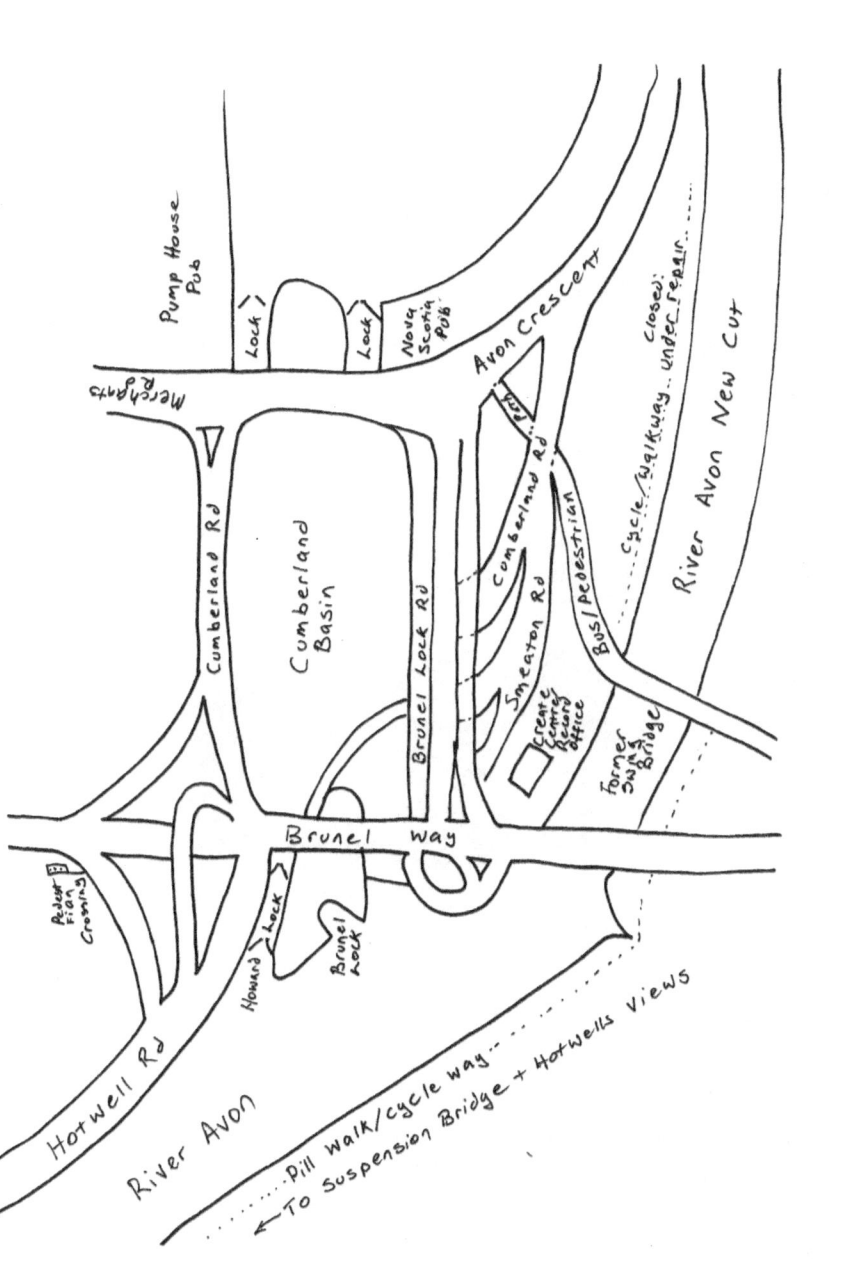

ELEVEN

Harbour and Hotwells

Start: Nova Scotia pub, Hotwells

End: Pill cycle path beneath the suspension bridge. Either retrace your steps to start, continue to Pill and catch bus back to centre, or climb Nightingale Valley to reach the suspension bridge

Length: Approx. 2 km/1.5 miles

Route: Main walk is completely flat, follows waters edge except for a few steps near the start. Optional extension into Leigh Woods is a long rocky slope which can be muddy.

Public Transport: Bus from city centre to Hotwells

CHAPTER ELEVEN

PREAMBLE

This walk deals with two important but very different aspects of Bristol's history which make the city unique: the maritime industries and the spa. Sailors heading to sea filled their water casks from the spring at the Hotwells and further downstream at Black Rock. This water was claimed to combat scurvy on long voyages. Hotwells was a primitive resort with basic lodgings in the seventeenth century. Its proximity to the spectacular Gorge and the Downs soon increased its popularity. From 1680 it gained a reputation for treating diabetes, but the Georgians used it mostly for treating 'pthisis', or tuberculosis. Honest doctors recommended it in combination with fresh air and exercise, which the region also provided. Charles II's wife Catherine of Braganza made a brief visit in 1677 while staying in Bath and so began its rise in popularity.

The Merchant Venturers purchased most of Clifton Manor in 1676, possibly to profit from the spring. They built an avenue of lime trees for promenading and the pump house. The resort became popular for the treatment of skin diseases, but came to specialise in treating TB. Visitors could cross the river for strawberries and cream at Rownham and Long Ashton.

The spa was always overshadowed by Bath, which was larger and closer to the capital. But the two sites came to complement each other, with different 'seasons' so visitors could migrate between the two. By the mid-18th century, the Hotwells summer season was attracting the rich and famous. Aristocrats and gentry drank the waters in the morning and went walking or riding on the Downs in the afternoons. Three large hotels and many lodging houses were full during 'the season'. By the 1770s the resort had grown to meet the expanded port.

A few years later the resort was abandoned to the invalids, and many businesses went bankrupt, with the blame largely laid on greed and overpricing. The reality was that George III had made Cheltenham popular, so the crowds followed him there. When Europe opened to travel at the end of the Napoleonic Wars, polite society abandoned the spa altogether. It was left to the terminally ill, so gained a reputation as a morgue.

Dr Thomas Beddoes was a respected reader in chemistry at Oxford, but he was interested in using gases to treat TB, so was attracted to the combination of ailing poor and wealthy rich to make a living there. He settled in Clifton, above the spa and founded his Pneumatic Institute on Dowry Square in 1798 to treat lung diseases with gases. He did not believe in the medical benefits of the spring. The institute employed Humphrey Davy, who made fireworks as a child and became a famous chemist and president of the Royal Society. Nitrous oxide was discovered at the institute in 1799 and was used to investigate the role of contagion in disease.

Southey and Coleridge were friends of Davey. They praised his skills and benevolence, and enjoyed strolling on the Downs, high on fresh air and laughing gas. Beddoes encouraged his supporters, such as the Marquis of Lansdown to fund a series of lectures on anatomy at the Red Lodge in 1797. This paved the way for the founding of Bristol's medical school in 1833.

A curving colonnade of former shops led to the now-lost Hotwell House. Ann Yearsley kept a library in one of them. She became famous as one of the 'uneducated poets'. She was known as 'Lactillia' as she was poor milkwoman who kept cows on Clifton Down. In 1784 she met Hannah More who encouraged her writing and helped gather famous subscribers for her publications. But they fell out over how to manage her money, and her career declined.

The main outlet for the spring is halfway down the riverbank, so Hotwell House was built into the river to protect it from the tide seeping in. By the 19th century, lack of investment, changing fashions and urban encroachment had sent the area into decline. Bristol's port expanded downstream towards the spa. Claims were made that it had destroyed the picturesque area and scared away the rich visitors, but fashions had changed. The fine boarding houses fell into decay.

Clifton was a tiny village in the 17th century. Alexander Pope recorded large houses under construction for wealthy Bristolians in search of fresh air. There was also accommodation for Hotwells visitors. Royal Surveyor Isaac Ware built Clifton Hill House for the draper Paul Fisher in the 1740s. Goldney House was largely paid for by profits from Woodes Rogers' circumnavigation. The original landscaped garden with gazebo and grotto survive. Both houses are now university halls of residence. The tiny country chapel was rebuilt to accommodate the wealthy residents and visitors. The area drew comparisons with Hampstead, and Montpelier in France.

This is yet another aspect of Bristol that is unique: the combination of a spa and a busy industrial city and port. Bristol's port was the main reason for its existence, but from the mid-18th century it was dangerously overcrowded. The rising port fees sent ships elsewhere, especially to Liverpool. The tortuous course of the Avon became more dangerous as ships increased in size. They were towed into port rather than driven by the powerful tide. When the tide went out, it left behind "an assemblage of nastiness". The levels of pollution from both human and industrial waste were overwhelming the river's natural ability to clean itself. When steam overtook sail, ships again increased in size to carry the coal they needed. Again, they found the narrow, winding, Avon increasingly dangerous. The first attempt at improvement was published by Mr Smeaton in 1765. He proposed damming the river Frome at the lower end of the quay, with the water diverted at he lower end of Canon's Marsh. But its estimated cost of £25,000, not counting the cost of land and losses to existing businesses could not justify its benefits. This was followed by a scheme by Quaker William Champion, cousin to the porcelain maker Richard. He ran the Warmley and Bitton copper works where he had built a dam to drive his mills. He built a dock near the city which was taken over by the Merchant Venturers and survives as Merchants' Dock.

In 1767 a scheme was proposed to flush out the harbour near the present entrance. This would provide a tide-free harbour, designed by William Jessop. The scheme enclosed the Cumberland Basin and enlarged Treen Mills pond to make Bathurst Basin. The tidal river was diverted into the New Cut, and the harbour was topped up by the Feeder Canal from Crews' Hole. This created 80 acres of deep water in the centre of the city. It was built between 1804 and 1809, and while the estimated cost was £200,000, it was eventually finished for £600,000. The first dividends were paid in 1823.

Some sources claim French prisoners of war were used to save costs. But this would have caused security problems, and there were plenty of men in need of work. It was built by a mix of Irish and English navvies, with the former doing the very heavy work. There may even have been an element of exploitation. Contemporary assembly lines sometimes employed nationals who hated each other. This inspired them to compete with each for from national pride.

The first vessels entered Bathurst Basin on 2 April 1802, and on 1 May the works were declared completed. A thousand workers were given a dinner near the Mardyke, with roast ox, potatoes and plum pudding. But after copious amounts of alcohol, a brawl broke out and the Irish retreated to their lodgings in Marsh Street for their shillelaghs. The resulting battle in Prince Street overwhelmed the local peace officers. The Riot Act was read and peace was eventually enforced by the press gang.

The new harbour created new problems. It soon filled with organic and chemical waste, creating a major health hazard and a shortage of clean water for drinking and industry. In 1832 Brunel converted the Overfall Lock, designed to power mills, to the Underfall, which allowed water to be emptied from the bottom of the harbour. He also introduced dredging to flush out the mud and filth.

Jessop's entrance lock was almost at right angles to the river, and the lock was too small for the new ships. Brunel was again called in, to build a wider lock at the Cumberland Basin in 1835.

After the disastrous 1851 wreck of the Demerera which blocked the river on its maiden voyage, action was at last taken to straighten the river. In the 1860s Thomas Howard built the present lock, much larger and better aligned with the river. The channel was deepened. Some of the more dangerous bends were straightened. Hotwell House was demolished and Hotwell Point removed. A tramway was built up the cliff to haul the spoil to fill the quarries on Durdham Down which had provided stone for buildings and roads.

THE AMBLE

CHAPTER ELEVEN   127

Start outside the Nova Scotia pub with its fine views of the harbour.

The Nova Scotia dates from the 1820s or possibly earlier. The name probably refers to the source of wood for the many timber wharves and shipbuilders upstream. It faces a mooring area for small boats, the original entrance lock to the floating harbour which was closed when Howard's lock was built. Opposite is a row of workers' cottages built by Bristol Dock Corporation. The first is home to the Merchant Mariners and is sometimes open to the public.

Cross the swing bridge to the Pump House pub.

This building supplied power to all the bridges and locks on the Cumberland Basin. For a time it was a slaughterhouse. Just upstream is the remains of a small bridge for the Port Railway. This ran from Temple Meads beneath Redcliffe Hill along the south of the floating harbour to end at Canon's Marsh. Pieces of old rails can be still seen in the area.

Cross the roadway at the end of the swing bridge and turn left to take a few steps down to the Cumberland Basin. Follow the water's edge to pass under the massive flyover built in the 1950s. Turn left to cross Howard's still functioning lock on one of the two sets of lock gates.

They are still in use so one or both of them may not be passable. You may have to wait or climb up onto the flyover to cross the water. This is a man-made strip of land, hence the subsidence of one of the buildings. Facing the New Cut is an indent on the water's edge. This is the remains of Jessop's original entrance. The other lock is Brunel's, and his redundant lock gate lies here.

Pass back under the flyover towards a huge anchor, to cross Brunel Lock Road, then under MacAdam Way to the carpark of the B Bond Warehouse and Create centre. Cross this towards the rusting bridge, the former Ashton Gate Swing Bridge which was replaced by the flyover, taking care to avoid buses. Cross the bridge and turn right into Greville Smyth Park to follow the Pill cycle path along the southern side of the river.

Almost level with the dock entrances is an information board. It provides details of the former Rownham Ferry. Visitors to the spa and, later, lesser mortals, crossed the Avon here to enjoy the beauties of Leigh Woods. They could visit the chocolate house and dine on strawberries and cream in season. Across the water, decaying piers show the former landing stages for pleasure craft and ships too large to enter the harbour. Small boats conveyed the contents of these to the city centre.

Along The Portway are former lodging houses for wealthy visitors to the Hotwells. Looming above the river on its massive abutment is Windsor Terrace. It was built by William Watts, inventor of lead shot, who was bankrupted by this project. Further along the water's edge a curving colonnade ends abruptly. In the late 18th century this promenade had a range of shops leading to the old Hotwell pump house which projected out over the water. It was the main part of the resort, and was rebuilt in 1822, but was demolished for the river improvements in the 1860s.

If the tide is low, the original spring can still be seen bubbling about halfway down the bank. A gateway into the rock face leads to the water-driven Clifton Rocks Railway which conveyed people up to the Victorian hotels on the heights. There have been many plans to restore it as a tourist attraction.

Next to this is an archway into the cliff face. Locals maintained their ancient right to drink the water for free in return for allowing the spring's enclosure for the resort. They were still drinking it here with the help of an attendant until it closed for health reasons in 1913.

Access to Clifton Down from Hotwells was originally via a track and steep steps from the rear of the spa house. This was dangerous in bad weather. Further along is the Zig Zag path, which leads up to the Suspension Bridge Lookout. Queen Victoria is said to have climbed it; she also climbed Scotland's holy mountain, Schiehallion, a real slog. In 1849 contractors were building four sewers for the city's western suburbs. They also built a second Zig Zag path between Clifton Down and the river. This is beyond Brunel's bridge and runs up to join Bridge Valley Road.

Opposite the Hotwells, a stream runs in a culvert under the path. In the 15th century William of Worcester recorded it as the scarlet well. It powered a small lead mill in the mid-18th century when visitors to the spa complained about its fumes. It was known for some time as the Red Mill. Like several others in the Bristol area, it ground logwood from the Caribbean. It produced a dye for cloth that was expensive but versatile as it changed colour in response to acidity or alkalinity.

Beyond the Suspension Bridge is a large railway tunnel. It was built in the 1860s for the Bristol Port and Pier Railway to Avonmouth, when an attempt was made to establish a resort there. By 1871 the port had silted up, and the investors made huge losses. It was always a local line, never linked to any main routes. The tunnel was apparently used as a bomb shelter by the BBC and by the locals during World War II.

After passing beneath the Suspension Bridge, you can retrace your steps to the start.

Or continue along the cycle/footpath to Pill where buses can return you to the centre of town.

Or turn left up the steep, rocky path in Nightingale Valley to enter Leigh Woods. There are many way marked walking and cycle paths here. It is a great place to see exotic dogs being walked and sometimes getting lost. Incredibly, in 1863 permission was given to build 350 tenements in Nightingale Valley, which caused such uproar that it was purchased for the public. Sometimes the authorities get it right.

At the top of Nightingale Valley, turn left onto the main road, left at a T-junction and to your left is the Suspension Bridge.

You can cross the bridge to the start of walk no. 12, visit Clifton Village or catch a bus back to the centre of the city.

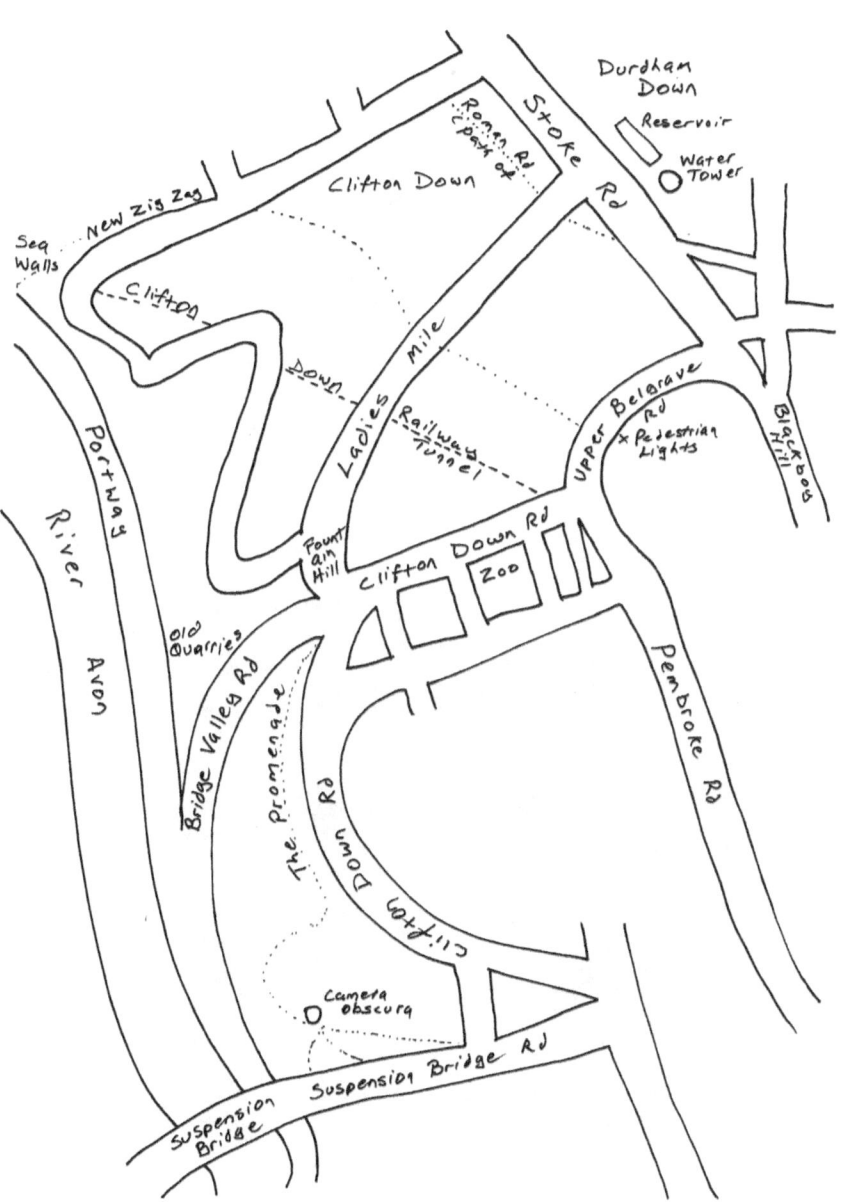

TWELVE

Up to the Downs

Start: Corner of Suspension Bridge Road and Clifton Down Road, Clifton Down
End: Water Tower, Stoke Road, Durdham Down

CHAPTER TWELVE

Length: Approx. 2.5 km/1.5 miles

Route: Undulating, partly on busy roads, the rest on parkland. Several slopes, one set of steps

Public Transport: Bus to start, return via bus from top of Blackboy Hill/Whiteladies Road

PREAMBLE

The Downs derive their odd name from the same origin as 'dunes'. The area was scrubby, windswept pasture for sheep. In the eighteenth century it was compared with the much larger and busier Hounslow Heath as a haunt of highwaymen and footpads. It attracted day trippers from the Hotwells spa. On public holidays, events such as boxing, cock fights and races attracted huge crowds of working people. From the 18th century, stone was dug on the surface for housebuilding, lime burning and road maintenance. In the 19th century, increased demand led to the digging of quarries. Old maps show rocky areas as being sites of lead mining. There was some surface mining, and accounts in local papers record miners gassing themselves while trying to smelt the ore. These traces were lost when the huge quarries were filled in and the area levelled.

During the Napoleonic Wars this was the site of an army camp. By the mid-19th century, overgrazing, quarrying, mining and encroachment by housing were putting the popular recreational area at risk. The corporation purchased both Clifton and Durdham Downs for the public in 1861. When the Cumberland Basin was built and bends in the river were straightened, the spoil was transported up the cliff by a railway to fill 3 of the 4 quarries. This explains why rocks usually found in rivers and seas are sometimes discovered here. The Bristol Dinosaur was found in a fissure near the top of Blackboy Hill in 1834, the 4th to be discovered in England. There were also remains of a mammoth and a lion. In 1842 a cavern was found in a quarry which contained the remains of bears, rhinoceroses, and wild bulls which were probably dragged there by hyenas. They were placed in the Philosophical Institute at the top of Park Street, but some were lost to war damage. The rest are in the city art gallery and museum.

The Downs have long been the site of an annual flower show, giant fireworks displays and circuses. The area has its own football league; at some clubs, 3 generations of the same family play together. It is popular with Sunday strollers, joggers, kite flyers and cyclists, and perhaps you, dear reader. On the Downs are small sandstone tombstone-like markers. They record the boundary between the parishes of Clifton and Westbury-on-Trym which developed along different lines. From the late 17th century, Clifton was owned by the Merchant Venturers who encouraged development, so houses on the west side of Whiteladies Road, which they owned, tend to be older than those to the east.

THE AMBLE

Begin at The Green, on the corner of Suspension Bridge Road and Clifton Down Road. Two monuments were erected by one of Bristol's many forgotten heroes, General Sir William Draper, who built nearby Manilla Hall, probably another Paty design, for his retirement. They have been so neglected to be now unreadable. He was the son of a local customs official and was educated at Eton. He was a soldier at Culloden and Flanders and then an officer in the East Indies. He led the defeat of the Spanish in Manilla in 1762 for which he was made a Knight of the Bath. He levelled the nearby ground near the Roman camp and found many Roman coins. Several local pubs were named in his memory. He was Keeper of the Downs, so was probably responsible for the earliest tree planting. He moved to Bath and then died in London.

A marble sarcophagus commemorates several of his battles including the taking of Manilla from the Spanish in 1763. This may be the country's first public war memorial. An obelisk is dedicated to William Pitt. The monuments were rescued from the grounds of Manilla Hall when it became a nunnery. The hall was demolished in the 1880s, with only the street to remember it. A monument to Elizabeth Draper by John Bacon Senior is one of the largest and finest in Bristol Cathedral, in its cloister. She was the model for Sterne's Eliza. It is unclear whether she was General Draper's wife or cousin-in-law.

From the monuments, stroll along Suspension Bridge Road. To the left is a former church, built by the Bridge Street Congregation when they escaped the city centre.

Cross the street at the top of Sion Place to the suspension bridge.

This provides great views of the Avon Valley. You can take a detour across the suspension bridge for spectacular views of the gorge.

Before the bridge, take the stepped path that veers uphill on the right near the public conveniences.

On the left of the path is a rock slide where generations of Bristol's children have deliberately torn their trousers to get new ones from their cash-strapped parents.

Pause at the top for glorious views of the bridge and gorge.

On the highest ground is the remains of a windmill. It was built in 1766, during nationwide food riots caused by grain speculation which were often recorded as famines. The mill was partly burnt down during strong winds in 1775 and restored as a corn mill in 1800 in the midst of a real famine. It was converted to an observatory and camera obscura in the 1830s by artist William West. He also dug the access to the Giant's Cave, a former hermitage.

Follow the cliff edge, then descend to turn left along Clifton Down Road and the tree-lined Promenade.

On summer evenings this is a good place to watch bats feeding. You can lie on the grass and have them swoop down low over you. Magic.

On the far corner of Canynge Road behind a high hedge is 'Elmdale'. It replaced the mayor's house on Queen Square, which was one of the first targets of the 1831 riots. This mansion was built by Alderman Thomas Proctor. He was the first importer of artificial fertiliser and the great promoter of the rebuilding of St Mary Redcliffe church. He also planted many trees along the south side of the New Cut in Bedminster. Proctor also donated the nearby Venetian fountain to commemorate the 1861 gift of the Downs to the public in perpetuity. A plaque on it states commemorates this important event. There is also a plaque recording its re-siting and refurbishment in 1988. The church, mansion and fountain were all by architect George Goodwin.

Continue along Clifton Down Road to the zoological gardens which had tragically been sold at the time of writing and their future in doubt.

They were originally planned to be on the Bath Road. Among the subscribers to the zoo were the city's great and good, including a certain I K Brunel. The original 19th century landscape by Richard Forrest is largely preserved, and the ballroom and tea pavilion from 1929–30 also survive.

Continue to the corner of Pembroke Road.

This was the site of the infamous Gallows' Acre for executions outside the city limits. St Michael's Hill was the site of the city's gallows until the New Gaol was built on Cumberland Rd. Criminals were often left hanging in chains and covered in tar to preserve them for months or even years as a warning to others. They attracted visitors from Clifton and Hotwells curious to see the bodies decay. Servants at local mansions complained the area was haunted and refused to go out after midnight.

Follow Upper Belgrave Road and cross at the pedestrian lights. From here you can veer left across the Downs to Sea Walls for spectacular views of the Avon and Severn.

In the 1750s builder and architect John Wallis built a wall here to prevent sheep and horsemen plummeting into the gorge. He wrote some cringeworthy poetry praising himself. The open space is popular with kite flyers on windy days. On very windy days it is a good place to see children being towed along by kites.

Alternatively, head towards the landmark water tower, skirting patches of trees and scrubland.

Following the first cholera outbreaks of 1832, authorities prioritised the supply of clean drinking water. From 1839 public drinking fountains were built on main streets. On the outer walls of churchyards, fountains reminded the public that Jesus was the water of life.

Near the water tower is a huge example of such a drinking fountain. It had metal cups on chains for humans, and troughs for farm animals. This fountain was erected in 1876 by public subscription of

100 guineas for the Bristol and West of England Agricultural Society's annual show. It was in anticipation of the Prince of Wales' visit to the event the following year.

The nearby ladies' conveniences were much used by members of the oldest profession. A plaque commemorates Victoria Hughes who was attendant there from 1929 till 1962. Her fascinating book 'Ladies Mile' records the story of how she "befriended and cared for" the women.

The Downs Cafe is beyond the water tower and changing rooms. It's a good place to end this long and probably windblown walk. It was formerly the men's conveniences.

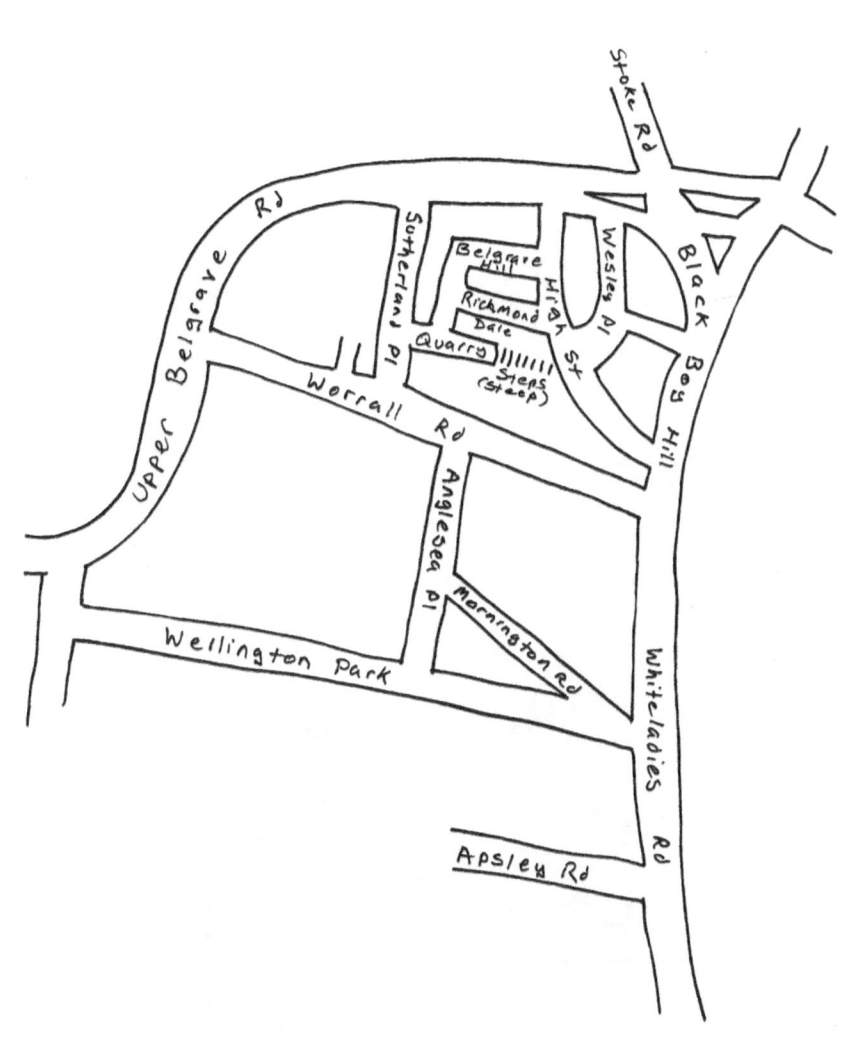

THIRTEEN

From Wasteland to Wealth

Start: Corner of Apsley Road and Whiteladies Road
End: Easter Garden, Blackboy Hill
Length: Approx. 1 km/0.75 mile

Route: Mostly flat, quiet streets. 1 gentle slope upwards
Public Transport: Buses on Whiteladies Road, Blackboy Hill
PREAMBLE

Three centuries ago Blackboy Hill and Durham Down were a wasteland: scrubby, windswept, and grazed by sheep and a few cows. Farmers passed through on their way to the city markets and it was also the road to the Hotwells' spring. The region was said to be as notorious as Hounslow Heath for highway robbers and footpads. But the area was much smaller and with fewer travellers.

From the late 17th century Hotwells became a fashionable resort. The Downs became popular for horse riding and taking in the air and scenery. On the far side was The Ostrich Inn, now a private house. It was so successful the owner paid for the Downs to be lit at night so visitors could return safely to their lodgings after probably imbibing a few too many lemonades. A rival venue with the same name was opened nearby for the less affluent.

Over the years, the Downs were popular for racing both horses and humans. Naked men won a cup, clothed women a Holland smock. There was prize fighting by both genders. Some of the best pugilists came from the Kingswood mining community. There were also occasional duels.

By the mid-19th century, the turf was being trampled and overgrazed, raising questions about the survival of the area. Sheepwalks were fenced in to become gardens, which were in turn built upon. Quarries by the river and on the high ground made the area dangerous for travellers, and heavy carts were ruining local roads. A travel guide described the drama of explosions sending rocks into the air but complained the area was being ruined. In 1861 the Bristol Corporation bought The Downs, and with the Merchant Venturers passed an act to make it an open public space. When the Cumberland Basin was built and the River Avon straightened in the 1860s, a tramway raised stone to fill in 3 of the 4 large quarries. The land was levelled in 1880. The remaining quarry held a tea garden, and was a site for rock concerts, then a private hospital. Grazing ceased on Clifton Down in the mid-19th century. It also declined on Durdham Down, eventually stopping in 1925.

The Health in Towns Report of 1854 listed Bristol as the third most unhealthy town in England. Whiteladies Road was a muddy lane with raw sewage running down the middle of it. Sewers and other improvements brought a better class of population into the area. As the quarries were run down, terraces and villas of local stone were built, often with Bath stone ornamentation. Good examples of both types survive, plus a few stables, workshops, etc off the main roads.

Many people believe the combination of Whiteladies Road with Blackboy Hill shows links with slavery, but this is nonsense. A Blackboy Inn was demolished when Whiteladies Road was built. Another of the same name was a popular venue lower down the hill. In the wake of the 2020 Black Lives Matter protests over Colston's statue, it closed.

The name's origin is unknown, though some suggest it referred to the swarthy Charles II. But nobody refers to a king as a 'boy' without risking their head. Before literacy was widespread, businesses used signs to attract custom. They often depicted exotic items such as foreign people, animals or fruit, to attract custom. A young black boy or an indigenous North American man was a popular sign where tobacco was sold. It was grown in England, especially in the Cotswolds but King Charles ordered crops destroyed as he made no money from importing it. The weed was still becoming established in the early 17th century colonies, so it was very expensive and sold in small quantities. It was smoked in tiny pipes which when found are often claimed to have belonged to leprechauns or similar nonsense. This is the most likely explanation for the name.

Crimes committed in the area were often tried at the Blackboy Inn.

Worrall Road is named after a dynasty of town clerks, bankers and property developers from the mid-18th century, several of whom were named Samuel. They owned the land now to the west of Sutherland Place. They planned to build on what was then considered open space at Clifton Down. But it caused great outrage and triggered demands for the area to be conserved. Squire Worrall of Knole near Almondsbury became famous for taking in — and being taken in by — the woman who claimed to be the exotic Princess Caraboo. Her portrait is in the city museum, and her story became a film in 1994.

THE AMBLE

Start outside the former St John's church, now auction rooms.

It is on the corner of Apsley Road, named after the Duke of Wellington's London house, which dates the area. As the quarries expanded in the 18th century, small cottages were built for the quarrymen, often within the quarries themselves. This made the houses hot in summer and prone to flooding in winter, and they also had problems with waste disposal.

Quarrymen worked hard, and had a reputation for being godless heavy drinkers. St John's church was built in 1841 for their improvement. It is a fine piece of Victorian magpie architecture, a mixture of Gothic styles, by S J Hicks. Its' octagonal towers resemble Holy Trinity, St Philips, by Hick's teacher, Thomas Rickman. By the 1850s the congregation numbered about 500, most of whom were attracted to the High Church preacher and were not locals. After World War II high taxes caused the rich to abandon the area, and many of their large houses were subdivided into flats.

Though its hall was still well used, the church closed in 1980, and in addition to the auction rooms, there is now student accommodation and a shop. Burials in the churchyard were banned in 1871, but bodies have not been removed. Three memorial stones survive, one to a family with an extraordinary number of children.

Head up Whiteladies' Road and turn left into Wellington Park to see a good selection of Victorian houses. Turn right into Anglesea Place, named after Wellington's cavalry commander at Waterloo.

A plaque on 29 Anglesea Place commemorates the birth of Randolph Sutton in 1888. He was a famous light entertainer, especially for his song 'On Mother Kelly's Doorstep' written for him and adopted by fan Danny La Rue. Sutton was also a friend of John Betjeman, was always immaculate in top hat and tails and was still working till near his death in 1969 aged 80.

On the corner of Worrall Road is the remains of an old Gothic style building, once a board school, which were schools built in poor areas. It was replaced by St John's school at the top of Blackboy Hill. But when traffic made that site dangerous, the present school was built here in the 1970s. By then the original school was ruinous, and most of it was demolished in 1974.

Until 1849 the north side of Worrall Road was called Caroline Place after Charles II which dates its construction. Caroline Cottage is one of several references in the area to the king (and also where the US state of Carolina got its name). Opposite was Island Place, a row of small cottages which is now the site of the school.

Turn into Sutherland Place to see on the left former livery stables on the edge of the old quarry.

Visitors to the Hotwells could hire horses here.

Turn right into Quarry Steps, then immediately left into Quarry Road. Detour half way up to the right along Richmond Dale to see an old brick building with 'Mission and Reading Room' spelt out in brick.

This is a fine example of Bristol Byzantine. It was built in 1870 by Redland Park Congregational Church which was active in helping the local poor. Reverend Urijah Thomas was its popular, hard-working preacher who spent his 39 year career working there. He was a hell-fire preacher who was so popular his church had to be rebuilt to accommodate the crowds. He is commemorated by the 1904 Grade II listed drinking fountain with shelter on the roundabout at the top of Blackboy Hill. He encouraged locals to visit poor parts of the city to run classes and sports for the needy, which benefited both groups. He founded a charity to provide food and shoes for the poor, which survives and still provides holidays for poor children. When he died in 1902 all the city's schools were closed for the funeral and 6,000 children lined the streets as the cortege made its way across the city to Arnos Vale Cemetery.

At the back of Upper Belgrave Road, a sheer rock face shows the signs of early buildings. These cramped tenements for quarrymen and their families were demolished in 20th century slum clearances.

Turn right up Belgrave Hill to see some fine surviving working men's cottages and the rear of the mission.

At the top of the hill is a small Gothic hall. Following the death of the workaholic travelling evangelist John Wesley, Methodism was split by schisms. Each group claimed to be Wesley's true followers. Wesley Hall was built by the Wesleyan Methodists in 1836. For several years it was home to the Moravians. They were pre-Reformation German Protestants who were associated with the Wesleys. They were very successful evangelists and travellers, who settled in most countries of the world. Their newsletters were probably the most widely read documents after the Bible.

Local directories show a bewildering succession of groups using this hall, and another was built in 1849 by the Reformed Methodists on Blackboy Hill. All these buildings and groups show how much need there was amongst the poor, and how much help was offered, but not by the established church.

Turn right into High Street.

On the left is the Easter Garden, a pleasant place to sit at the end of this walk. This has been the focus of a long-running battle between local residents who wanted it preserved as a green space, and a series of developers who wanted to build on it. The locals have won awards and grants for building and maintaining this small community garden.

REFERENCES/FURTHER READING

William Barratt, The History and Antiquities of the City of Bristol
Andrew Foyle, Bristol, Pevsner Architectural Guides
John Latimer, The Annals of Bristol vols 1-3,
Bryan Little, The City and County of Bristol
J F Nicholls & John Taylor, Bristol Past and Present, Vol. 3
Nicholas Pevsner, North Somerset and Bristol, The Buildings of England series
Various publications and scribbled notes by the author

ABOUT THE AUTHOR

Barb Drummond lived in Bristol for many years and since 2005 she has self published history books on a wide range of topics. She was commissioned by the British Empire and Commonwealth Museum to conduct research for the bicentenary of the Abolition of the Slave Trade Act in 2007 and has given talks, led walks and appeared on radio and local tv.

    She can be contacted on Facebook,
    twitter: @Barb_Drummond
    email: texthistory.outlook.com

www.ingramcontent.com/pod-product-compliance
Lightning Source LLC
Chambersburg PA
CBHW030259100526
44590CB00012B/450